City People Notebook

The Will Eisner Library

Hardcover Compilations

The Contract With God *Trilogy*
Will Eisner's New York
Life, in Pictures

Paperbacks

A Contract With God
A Life Force
New York: The Big City
Will Eisner Reader
The Dreamer
Invisible People
To the Heart of the Storm
Dropsie Avenue
Life on Another Planet
Family Matter
Minor Miracles
Name of the Game
The Building
The Plot: The Secret Story of the Protocols of the Elders of Zion

Instructional Textbooks

Comics and Sequential Art
Graphic Storytelling and Visual Narrative
Expressive Anatomy for Comics and Narrative

Other Books by Will Eisner

Fagin the Jew
Last Day in Vietnam
Eisner/Miller
The Spirit Archives
Will Eisner Sketchbook
Will Eisner's Shop Talk
Hawks of the Seas
The Princess and the Frog
The Last Knight
Moby Dick
Sundiata

City People
Notebook

Will Eisner

W. W. NORTON & COMPANY
New York • London

ACKNOWLEDGEMENT

To Dave Schreiner, my gratitude for his solid editorial support. To Cat Yronwode who, as she has so often in the past, contributed valuable insight and candid comments — my appreciation.

For information about permission to reproduce selections from this book, write to
Permissions, W. W. Norton & Company, Inc., 500 Fifth Avenue, New York, NY 10110

Manufacturing by RR Donnelley, Willard
Production manager: Devon Zahn and Joe Lops

The Library of Congress has cataloged the one-volume edition as follows:
Eisner, Will.
[Selections. 2006]
Will Eisner's New York : life in the big city / Will Eisner ; introduction by Neil Gaiman.
p. cm. — (The Will Eisner library)
Four graphic novels, originally published 1987–2000 by various publishers.
Contents: New York : the big city— The building—City people
notebook —Invisible people.
ISBN 13: 978-0-393-06106-2
ISBN 10: 0-393-06106-X
1. Graphic novels. I. Title. II. Title: New York, life in the big city.

PN6727.E4A6 2006
741.5—dc22
2006046674

ISBN 978-0-393-32806-6 pbk.

W. W. Norton & Company, Inc.
500 Fifth Avenue, New York, N.Y. 10110
www.wwnorton.com

W. W. Norton & Company Ltd.
Castle House, 75/76 Wells Street, London W1T 3QT

1 2 3 4 5 6 7 8 9 0

New Introduction to
City People Notebook

LIVING IN A BIG CITY
CAN BE COMPARED
TO EXISTING IN A JUNGLE.
ONE BECOMES A
CREATURE OF THE
ENVIRONMENT.
THE RESPONSE TO THE
RHYTHMS AND CHOREOGRAPHY
IS VISCERAL
AND BEFORE LONG
A DWELLER'S CONDUCT IS
AS DISTINCTIVE AS
THOSE OF A
JUNGLE INHABITANT.
ARCANE SURVIVAL
SKILLS AND SUBTLE
PERSONALITY CHANGES
TAKE PLACE THAT
AFFECT BEHAVIOR.
HEREIN IS A KIND OF
ARCHAEOLOGICAL
STUDY OF CITY PEOPLE.

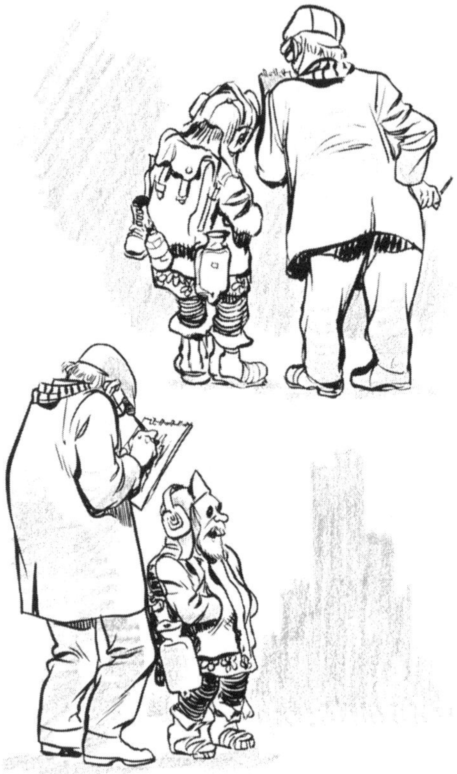

TO ME,
CITY PEOPLE
HAVE ALWAYS
SEEMED SINGULAR
IN STYLE AND
SENSIBILITIES.
CLEARLY, LIFE
DEEP IN A BIG
CITY IS VERY
DIFFERENT
THAN THAT
OF A SMALL
RURAL
COMMUNITY.
AS THE
STREET SMARTS
AND SURVIVAL
SKILLS ARE
ACCUMULATED,
IT AFFIRMS
ENVIRONMENT'S
TRIUMPH OVER
US ALL.

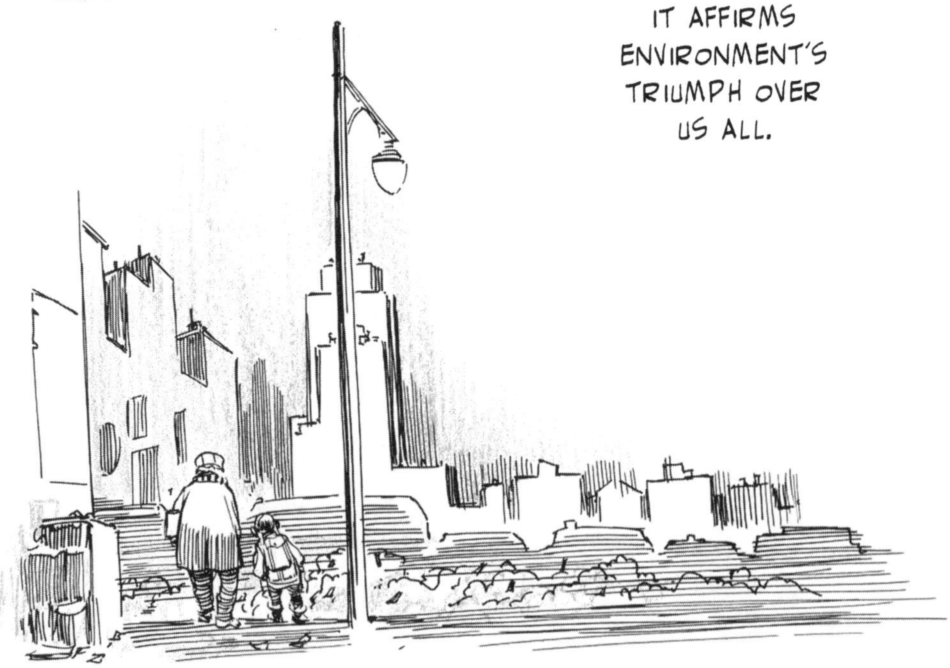

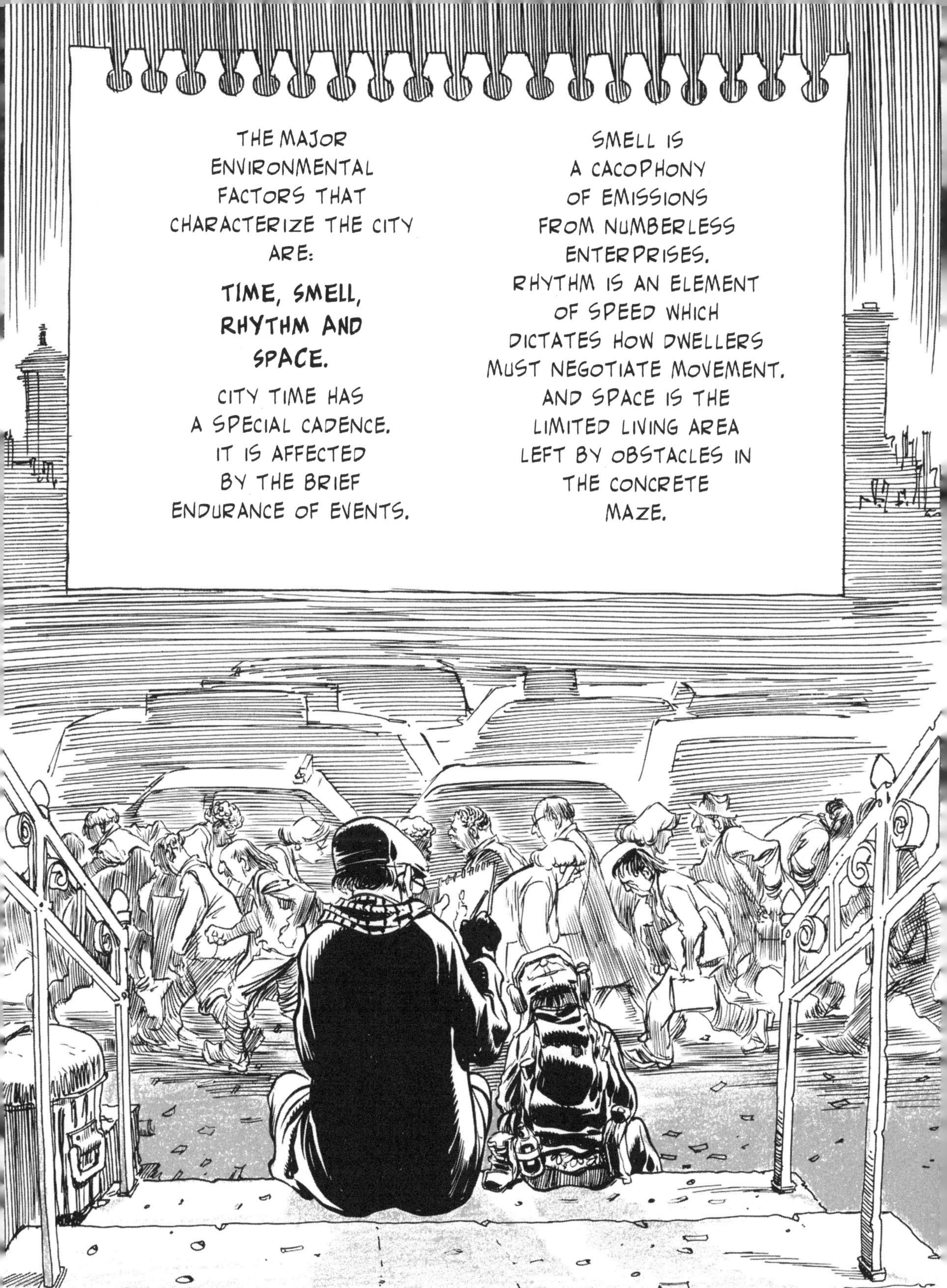
THE MAJOR ENVIRONMENTAL FACTORS THAT CHARACTERIZE THE CITY ARE:
TIME, SMELL, RHYTHM AND SPACE.
CITY TIME HAS A SPECIAL CADENCE. IT IS AFFECTED BY THE BRIEF ENDURANCE OF EVENTS.
SMELL IS A CACOPHONY OF EMISSIONS FROM NUMBERLESS ENTERPRISES.
RHYTHM IS AN ELEMENT OF SPEED WHICH DICTATES HOW DWELLERS MUST NEGOTIATE MOVEMENT.
AND SPACE IS THE LIMITED LIVING AREA LEFT BY OBSTACLES IN THE CONCRETE MAZE.

CITY PEOPLE

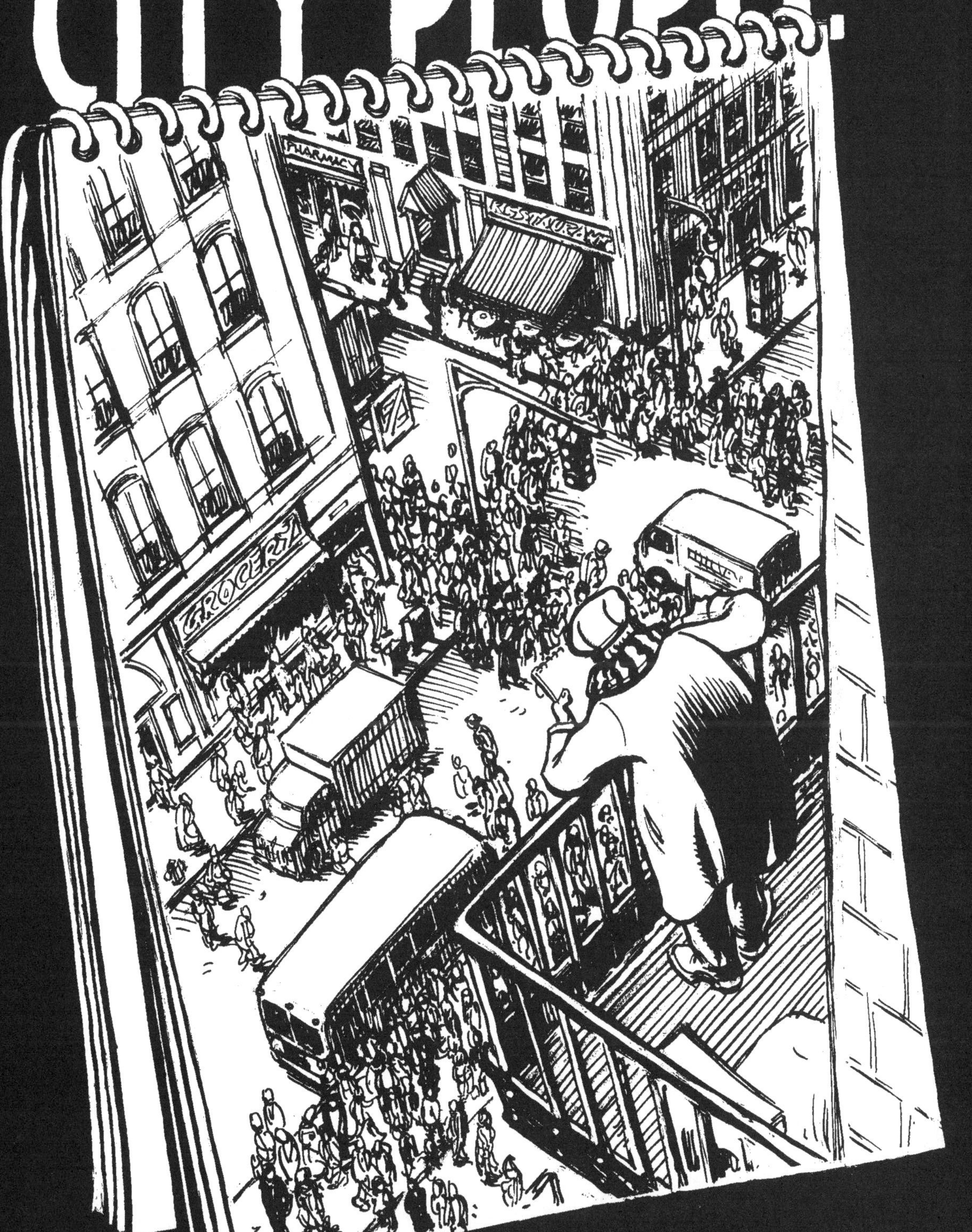
PHARMACY
GROCERY

ON-TIMESMANSHIP

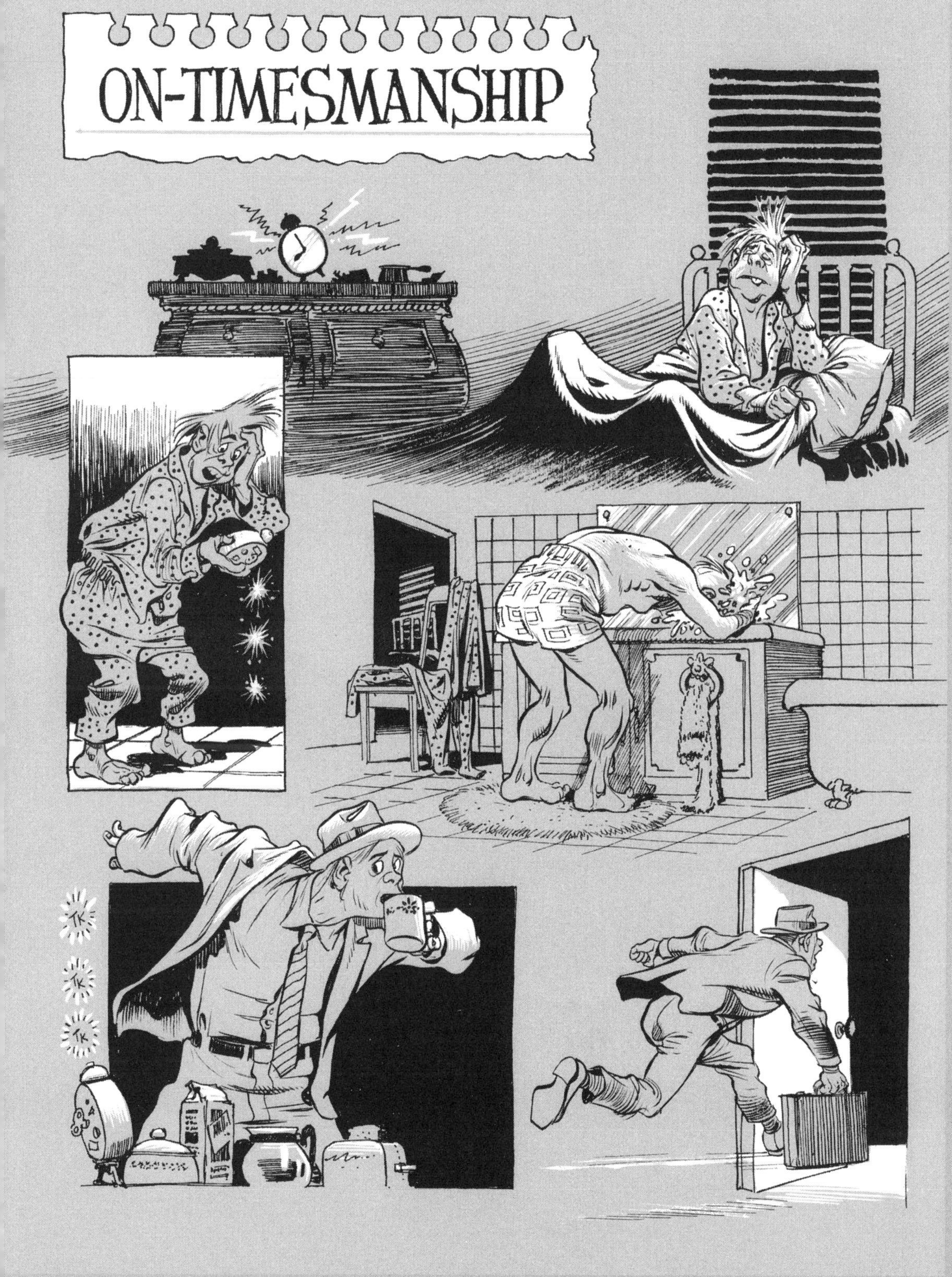
TK
TK
TK

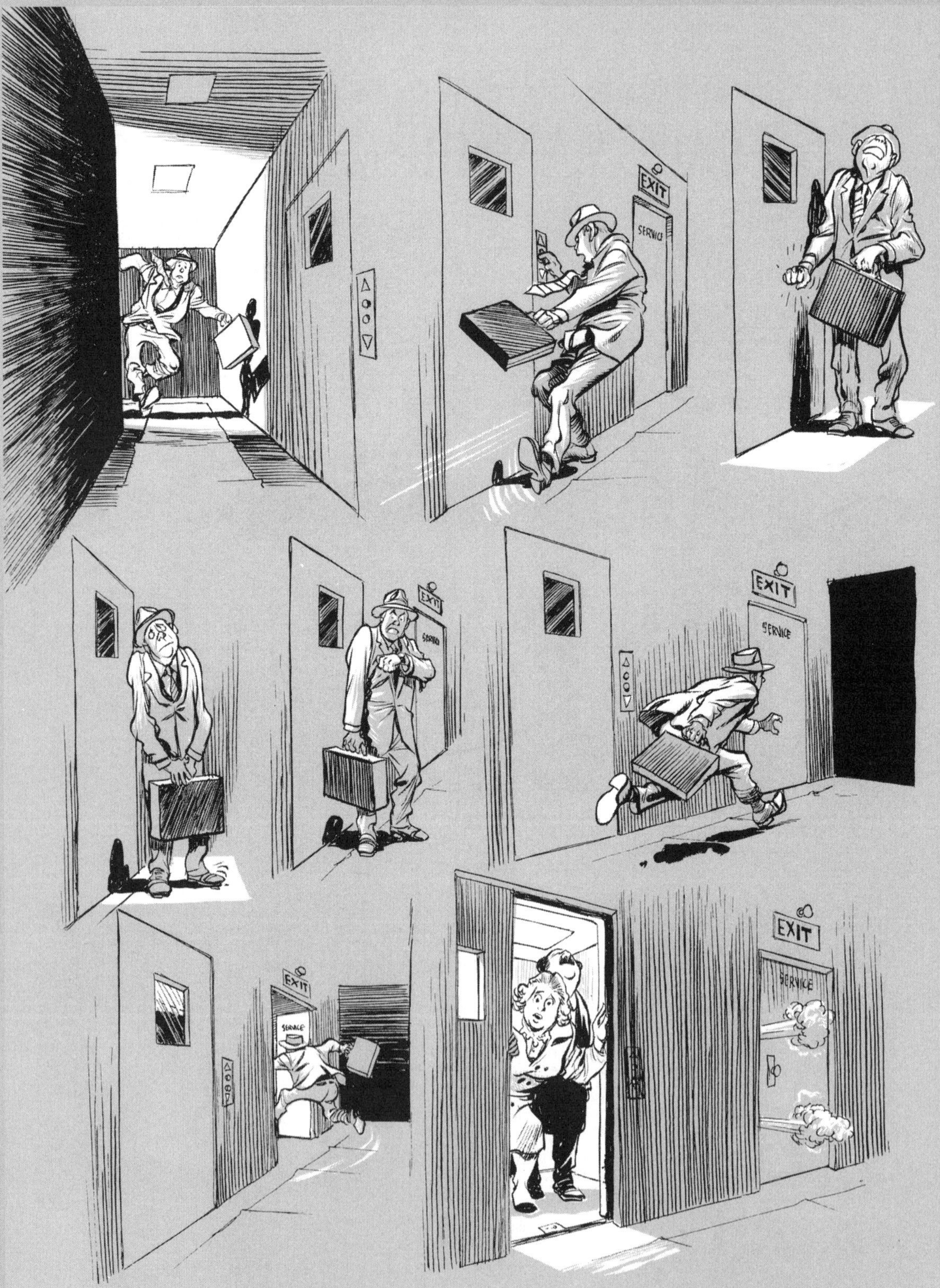
EXIT
SERVICE
EXIT
SERVICE
EXIT
SERVICE
EXIT
SERVICE

!!
!!
DOWNTO
!?
TOKENS

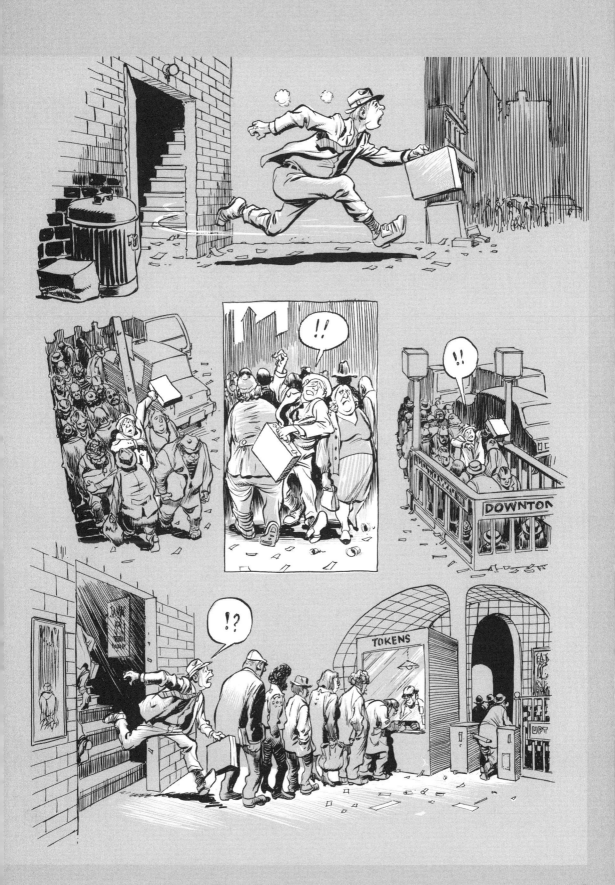

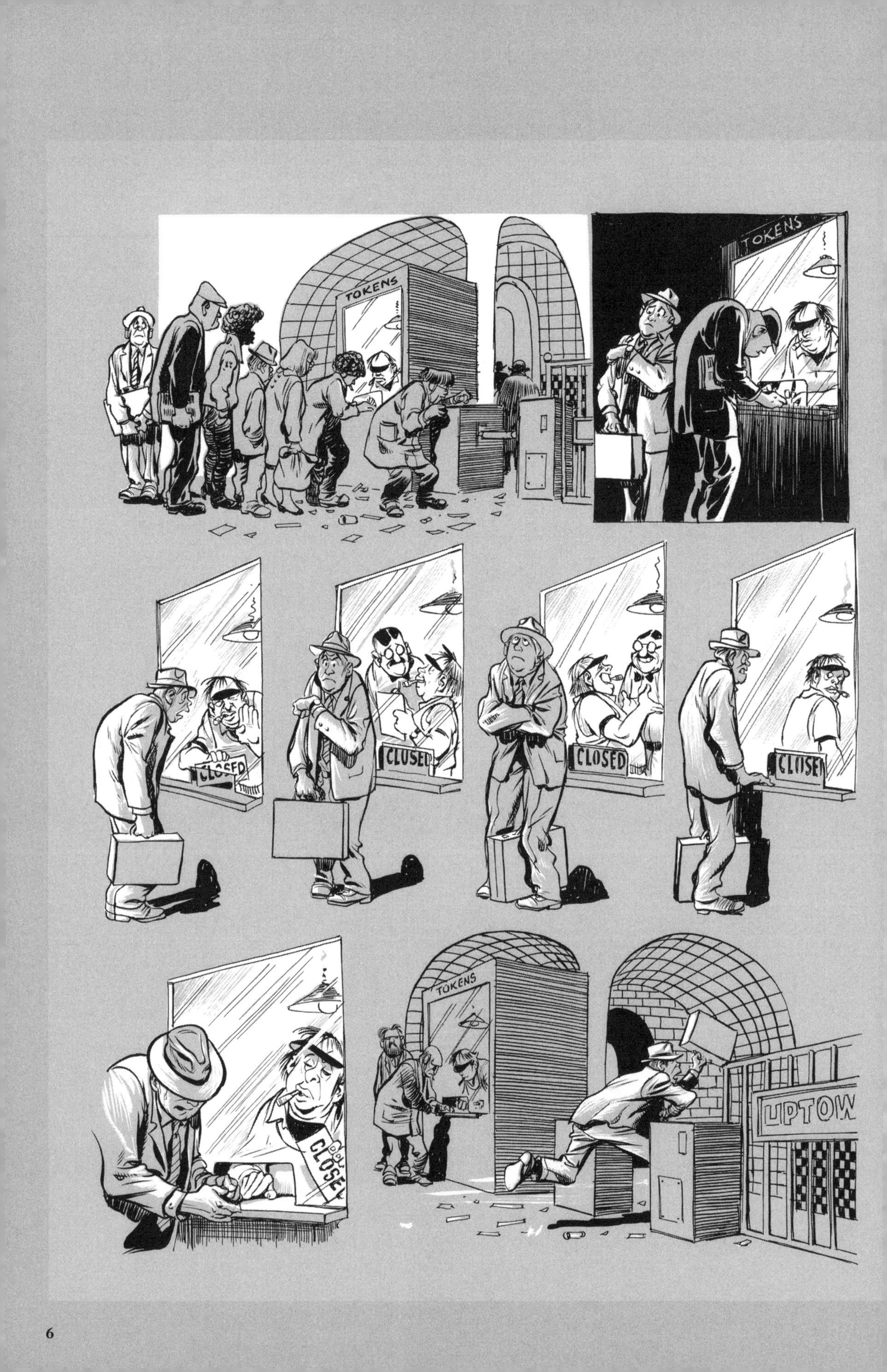
TOKENS
TOKENS
CLOSED
CLOSED
CLOSED
TOKENS
UPTOW

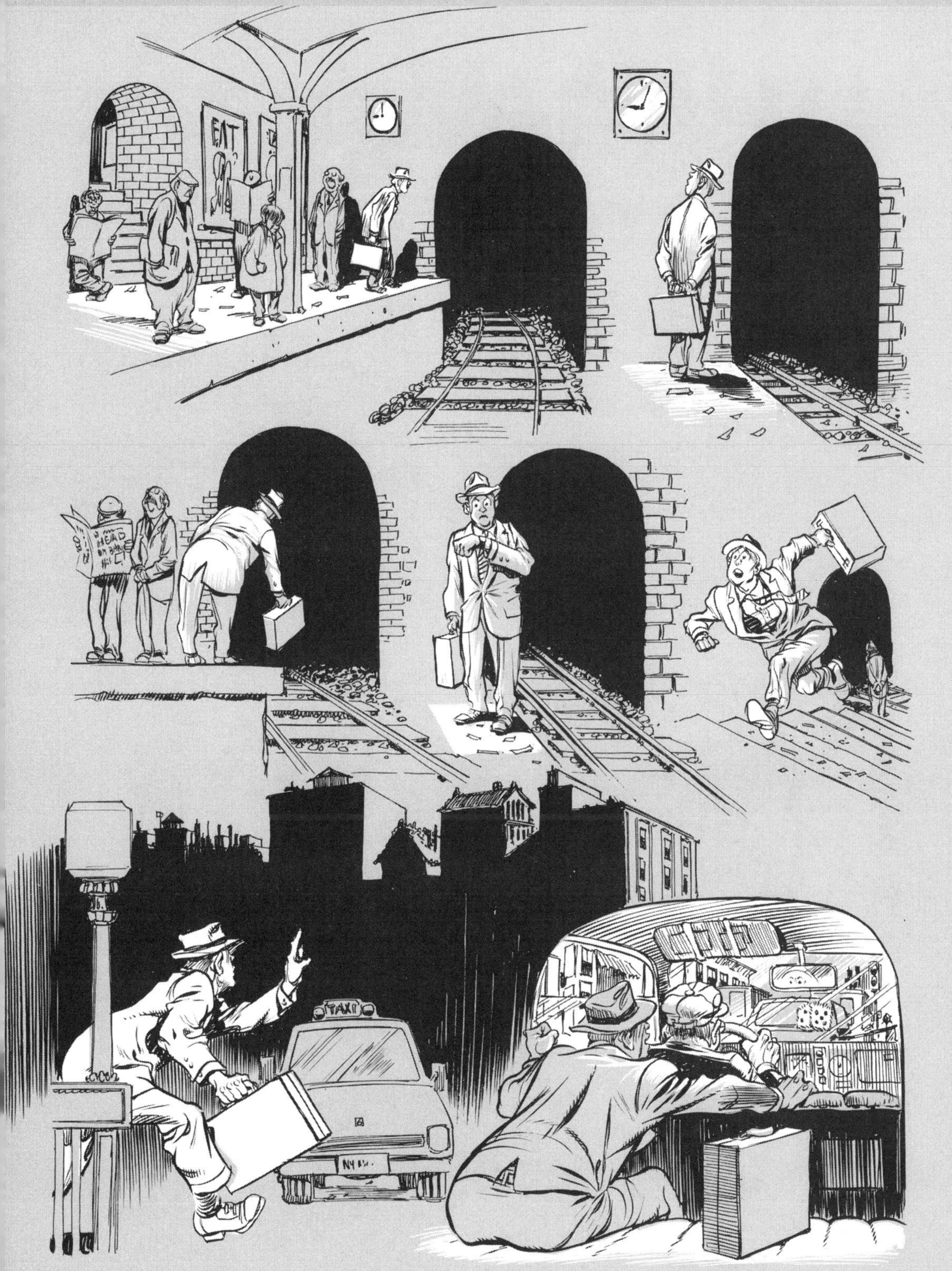
EAT
HEAD
TAXI

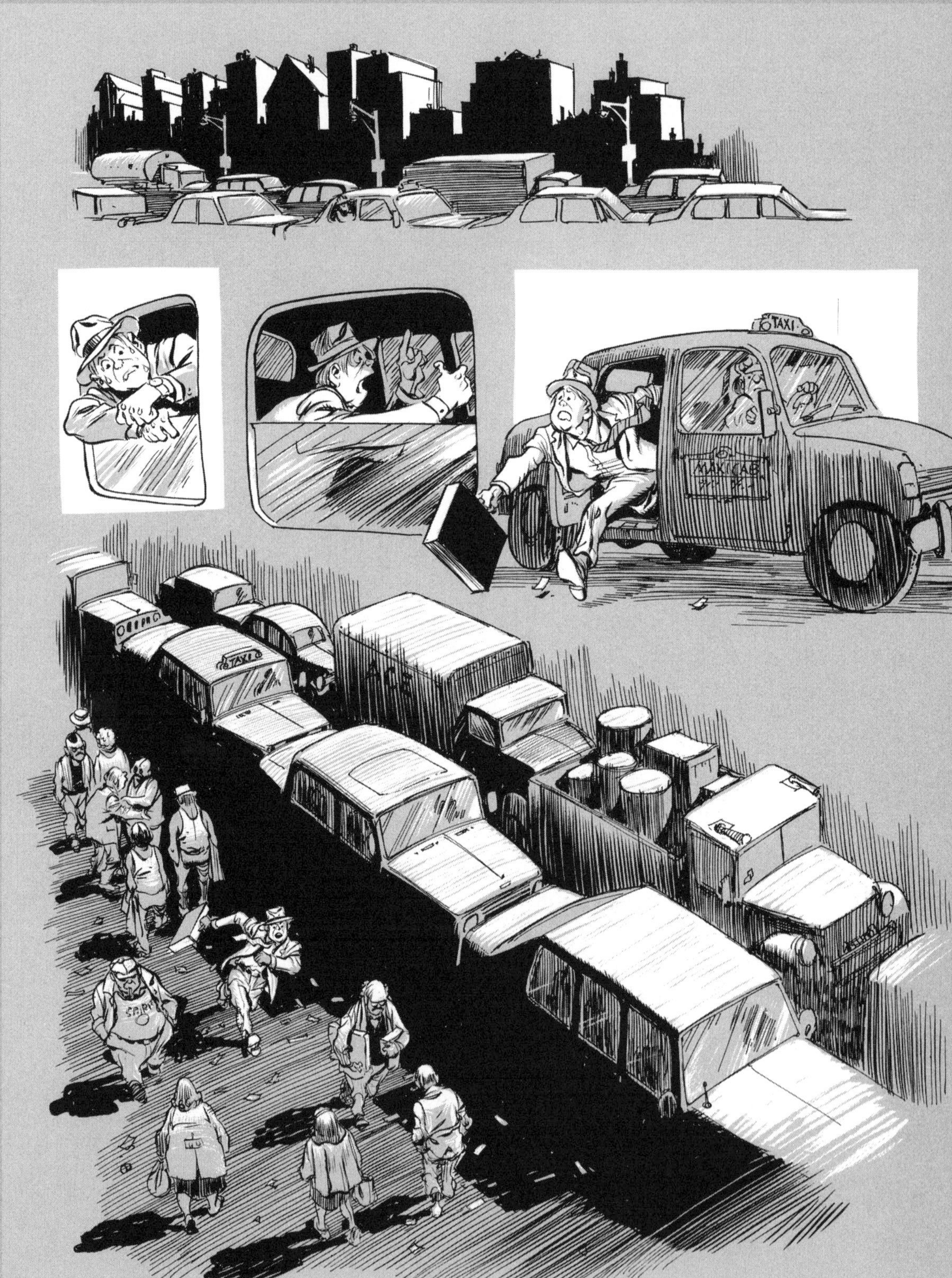
TAXI
MAXICAB
TAXI
ACE

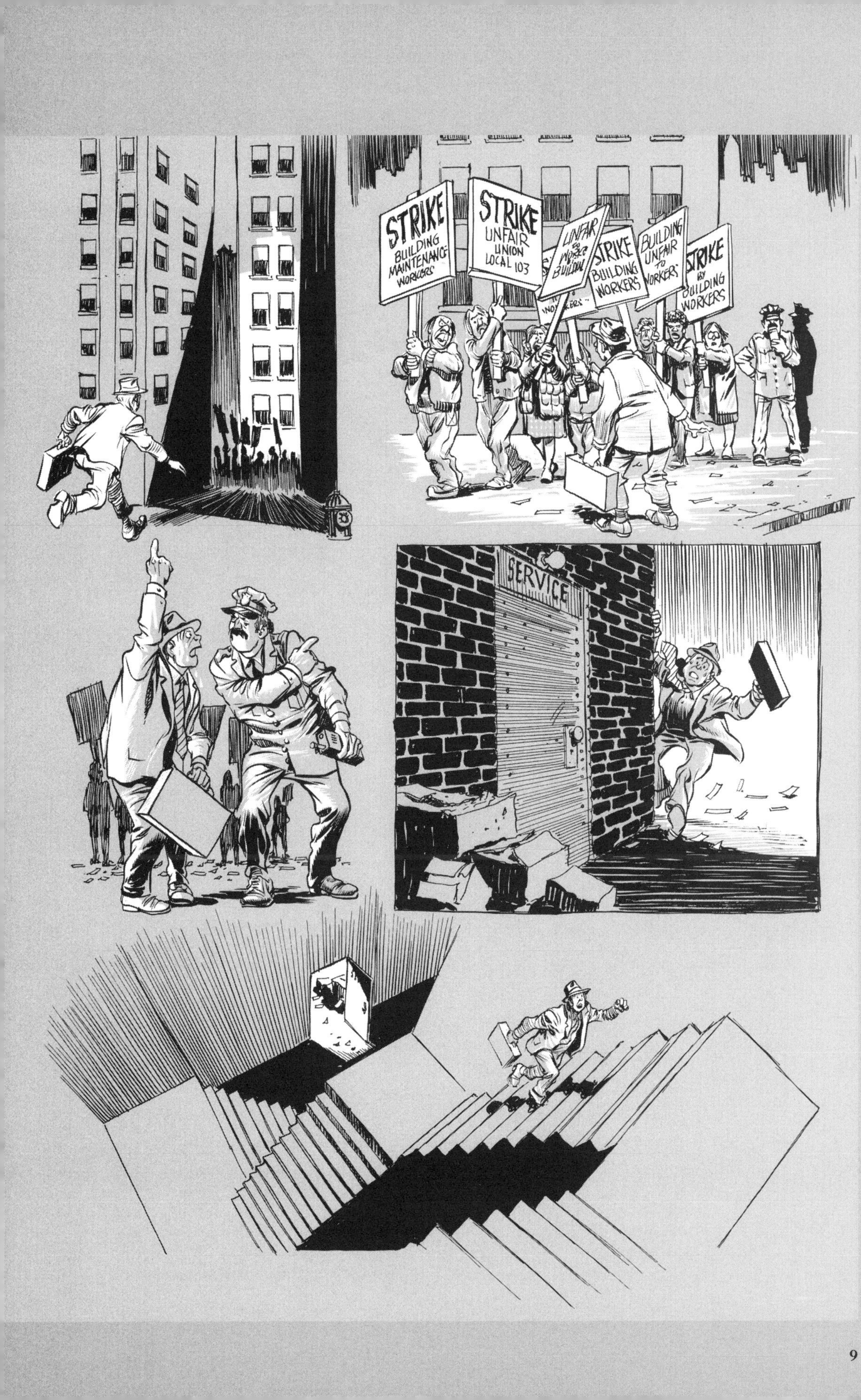
STRIKE BUILDING MAINTENANCE WORKERS
STRIKE UNFAIR UNION LOCAL 103
UNFAIR
STRIKE BUILDING WORKERS
BUILDING UNFAIR TO WORKERS
STRIKE BY BUILDING WORKERS
SERVICE

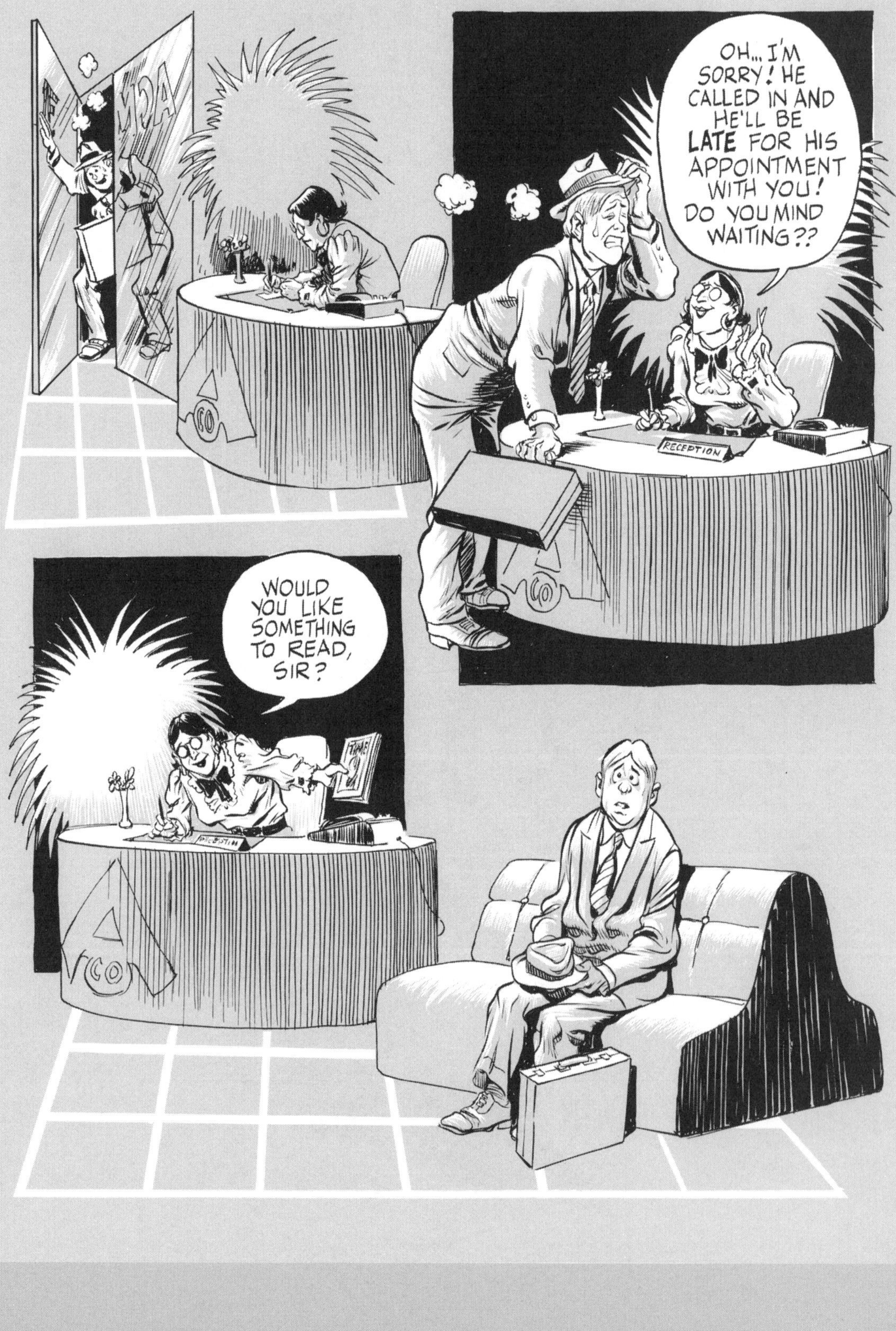

OH... I'M SORRY! HE CALLED IN AND HE'LL BE LATE FOR HIS APPOINTMENT WITH YOU! DO YOU MIND WAITING??
RECEPTION
WOULD YOU LIKE SOMETHING TO READ, SIR?

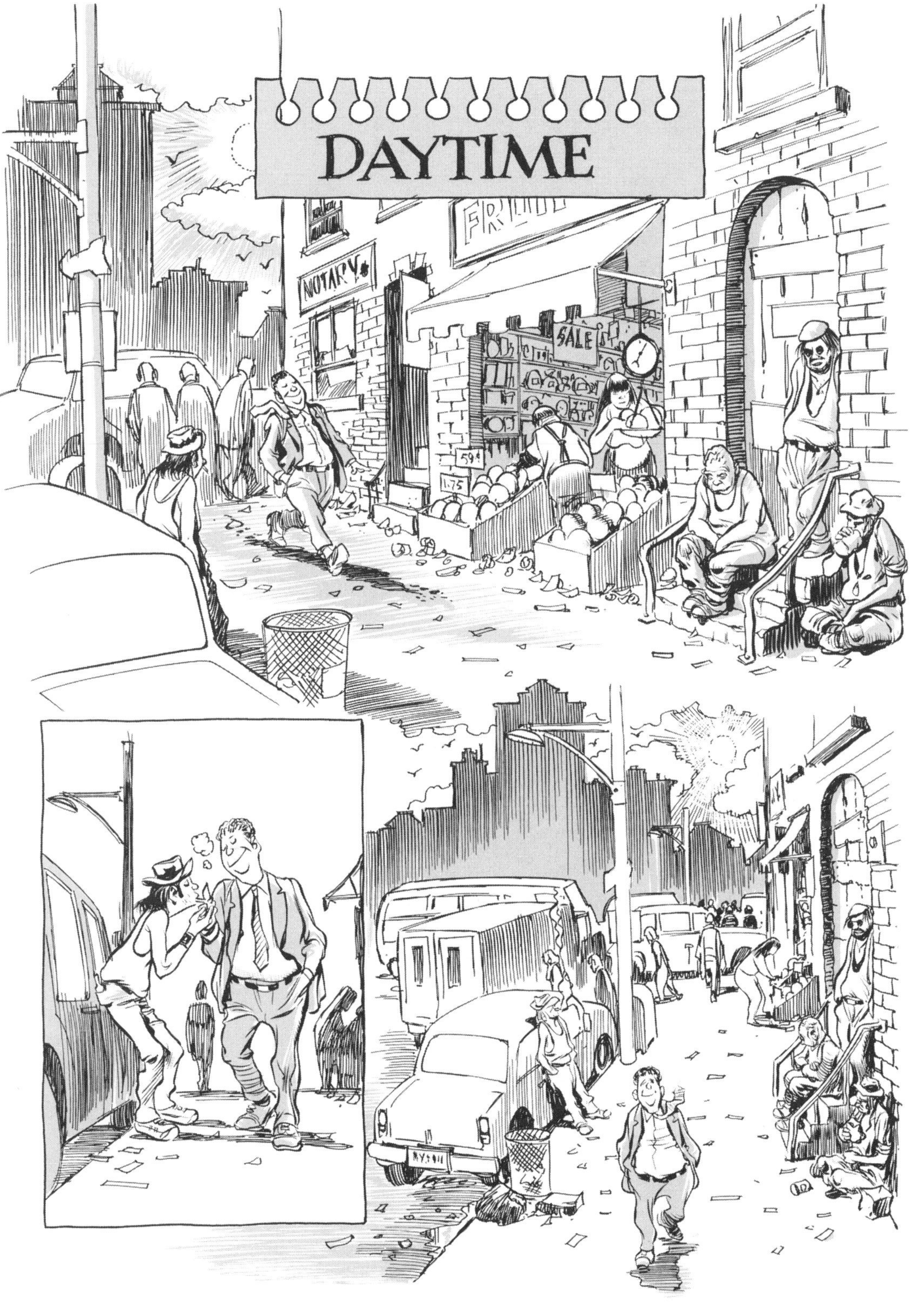
DAYTIME
NOTARY
SALE
59¢
1.75

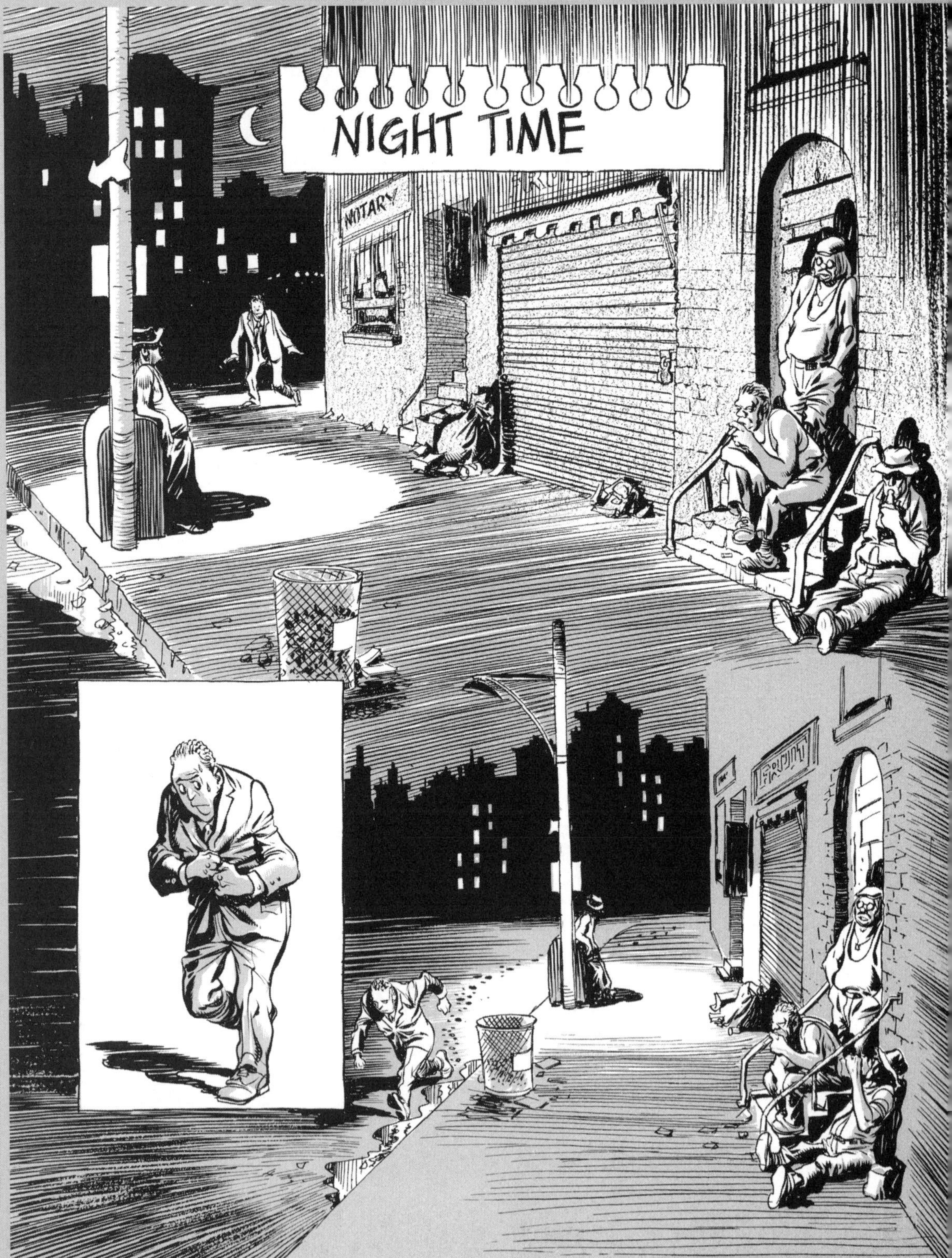
NIGHT TIME
NOTARY

LIFE TIME
SOAP POWDER ACTOR
TAXI
ACE

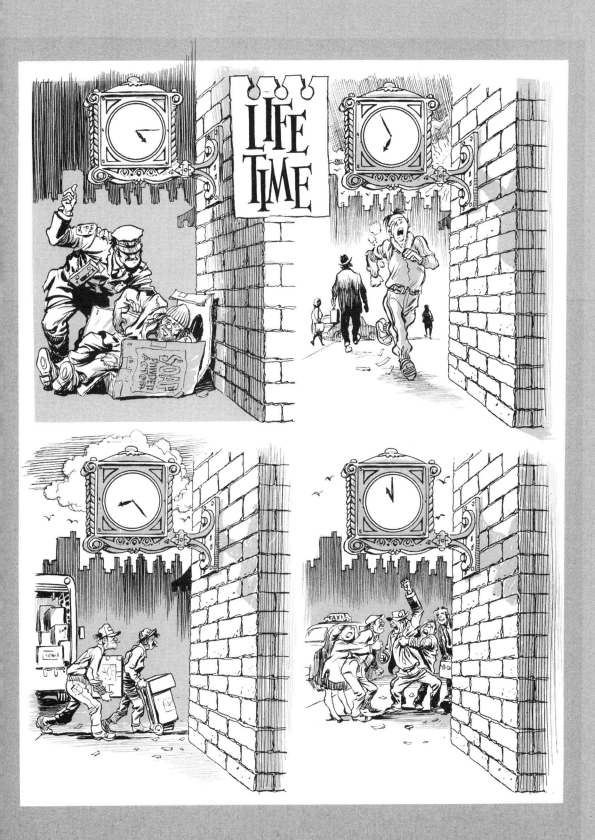

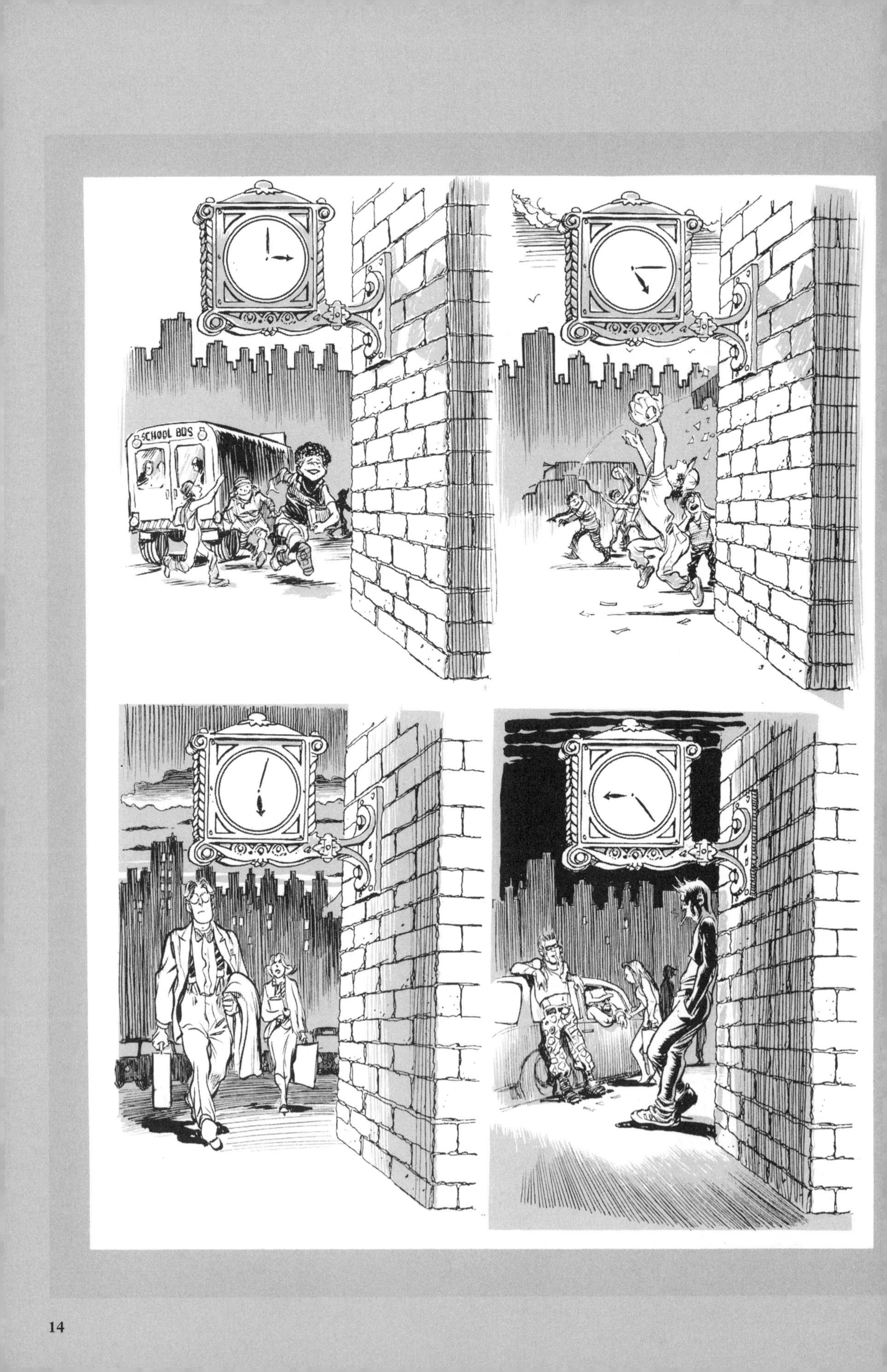
SCHOOL BUS

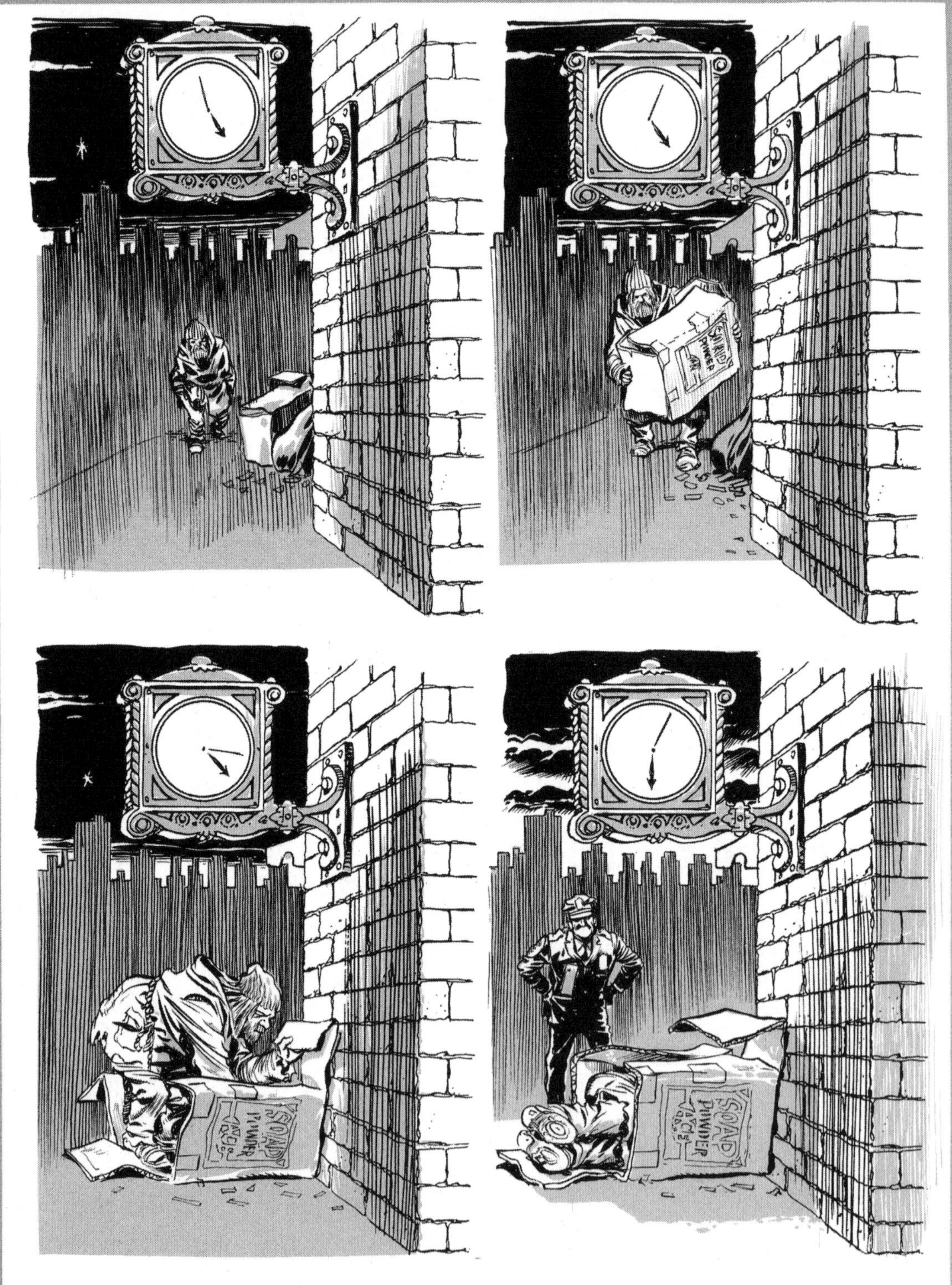

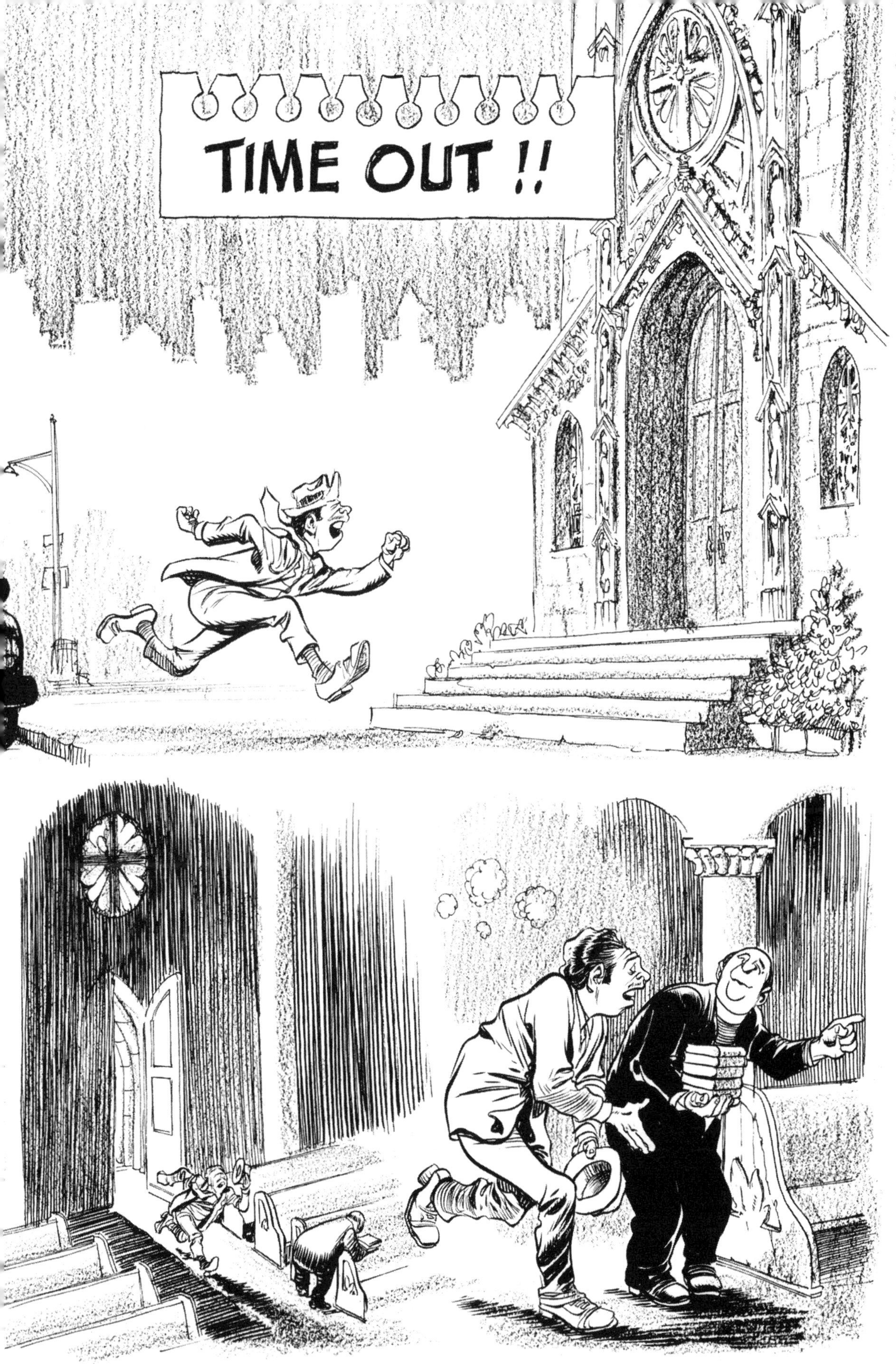
TIME OUT !!

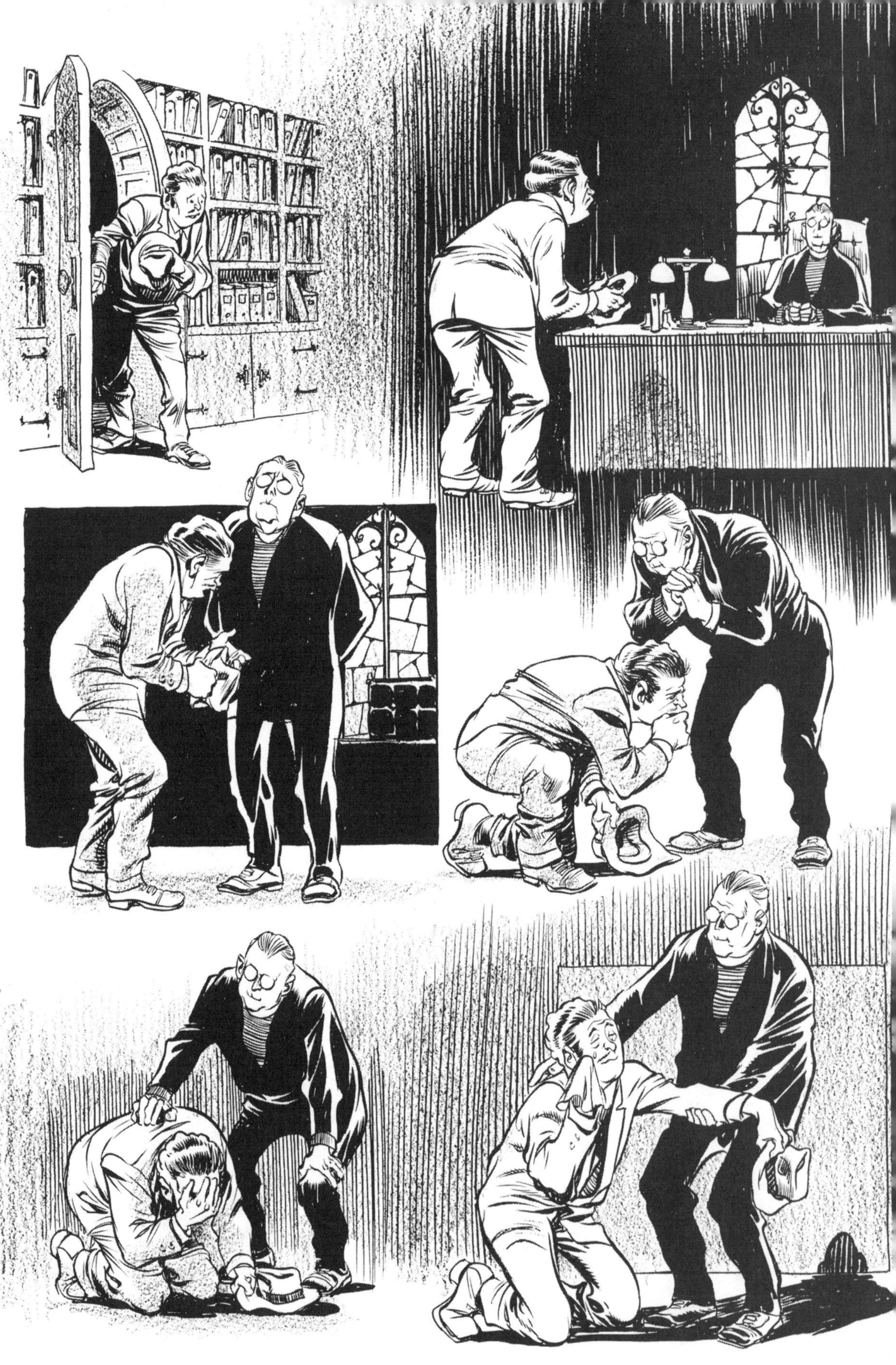

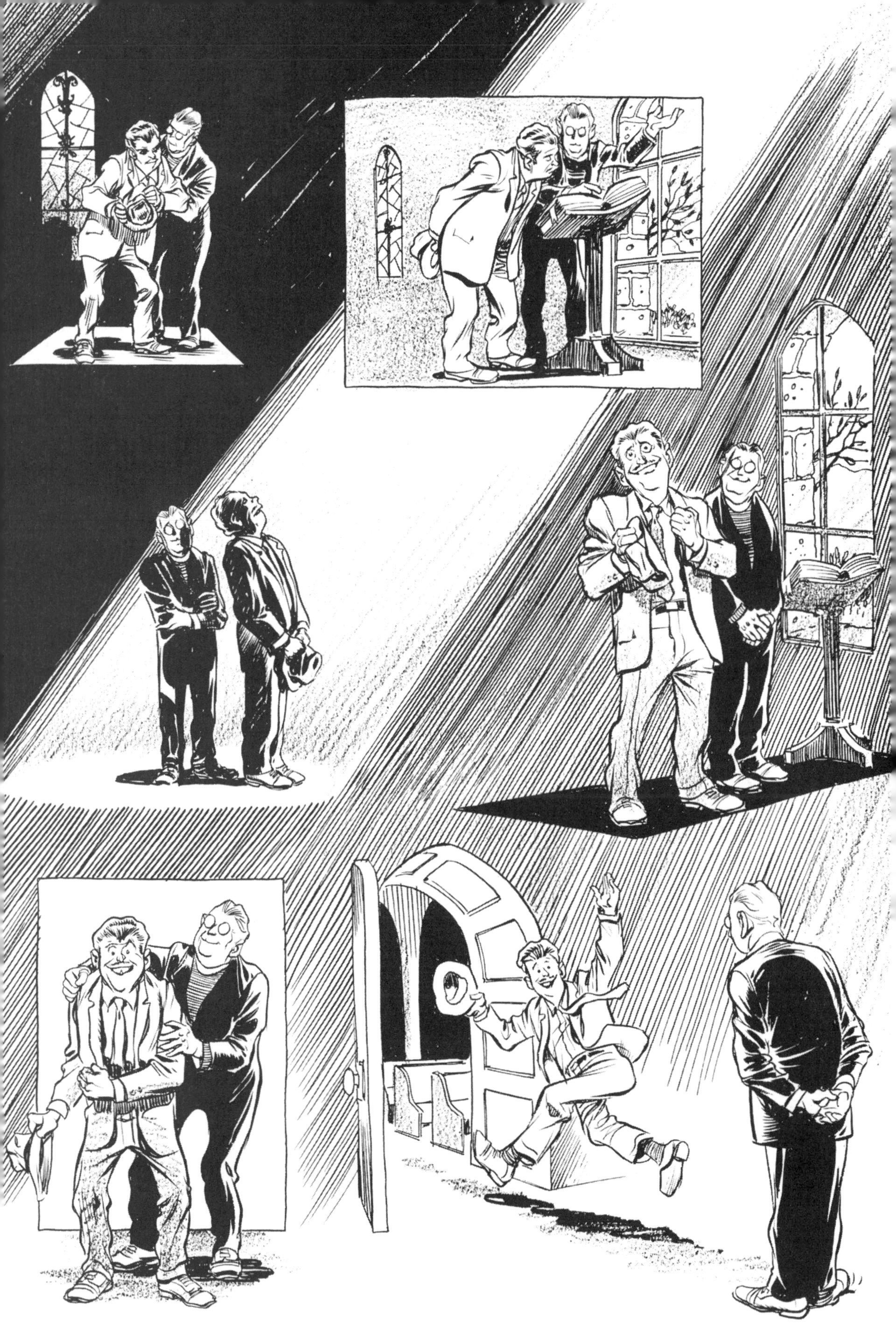

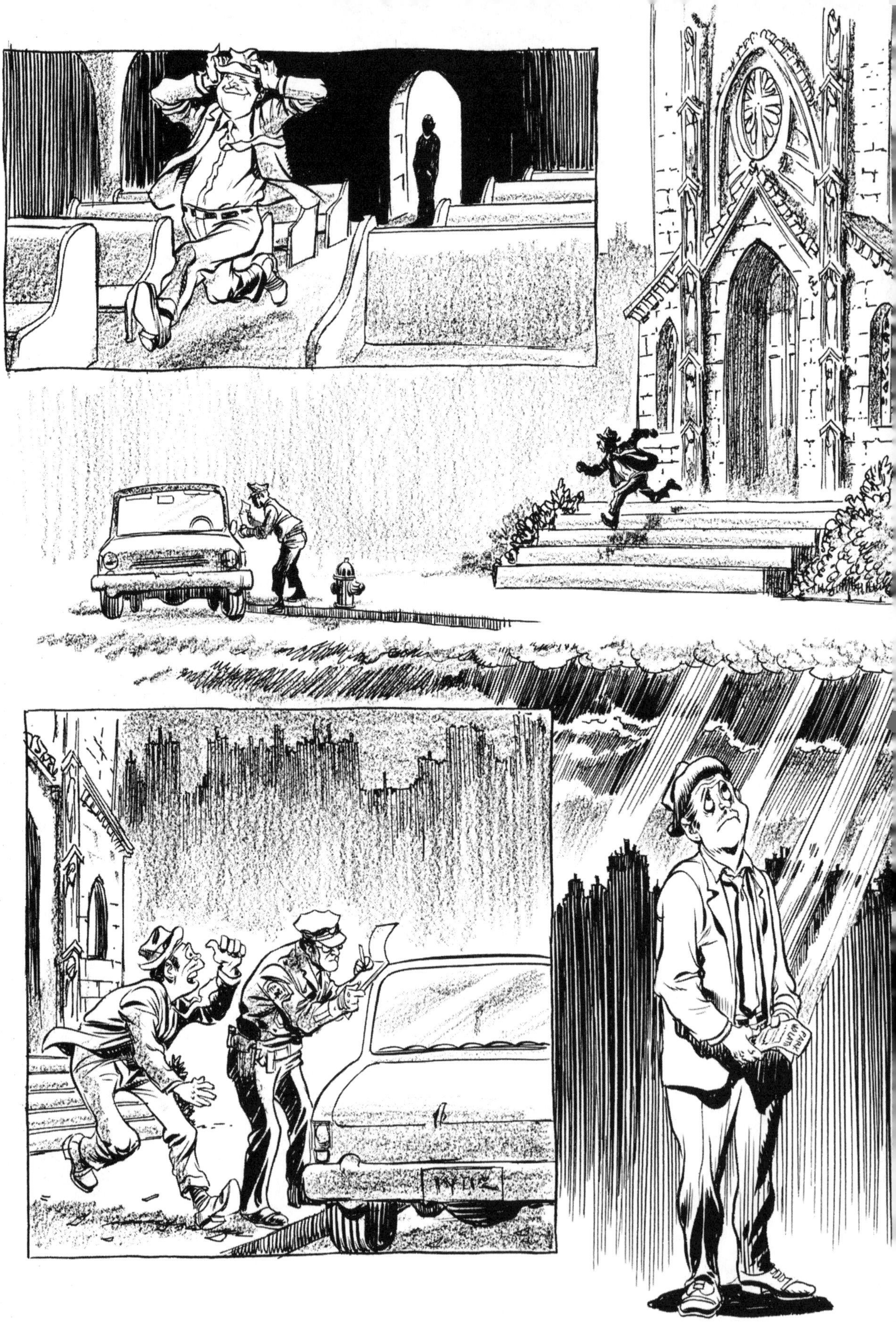
PARK

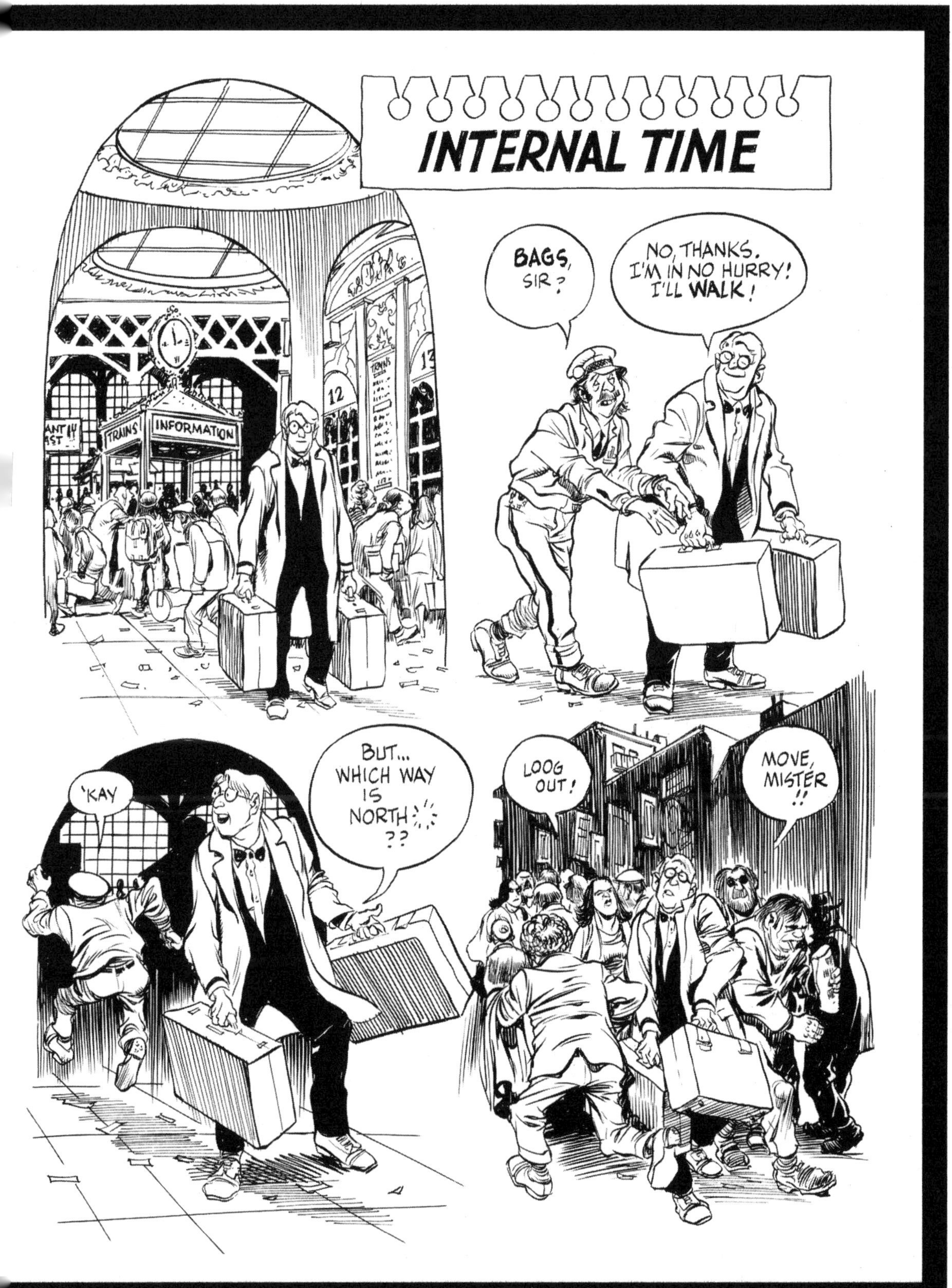
INTERNAL TIME
TRAINS
INFORMATION
12
13
TRAINS
BAGS, SIR?
NO, THANKS. I'M IN NO HURRY! I'LL WALK!
'KAY
BUT... WHICH WAY IS NORTH ??
LOOG OUT!
MOVE, MISTER !!

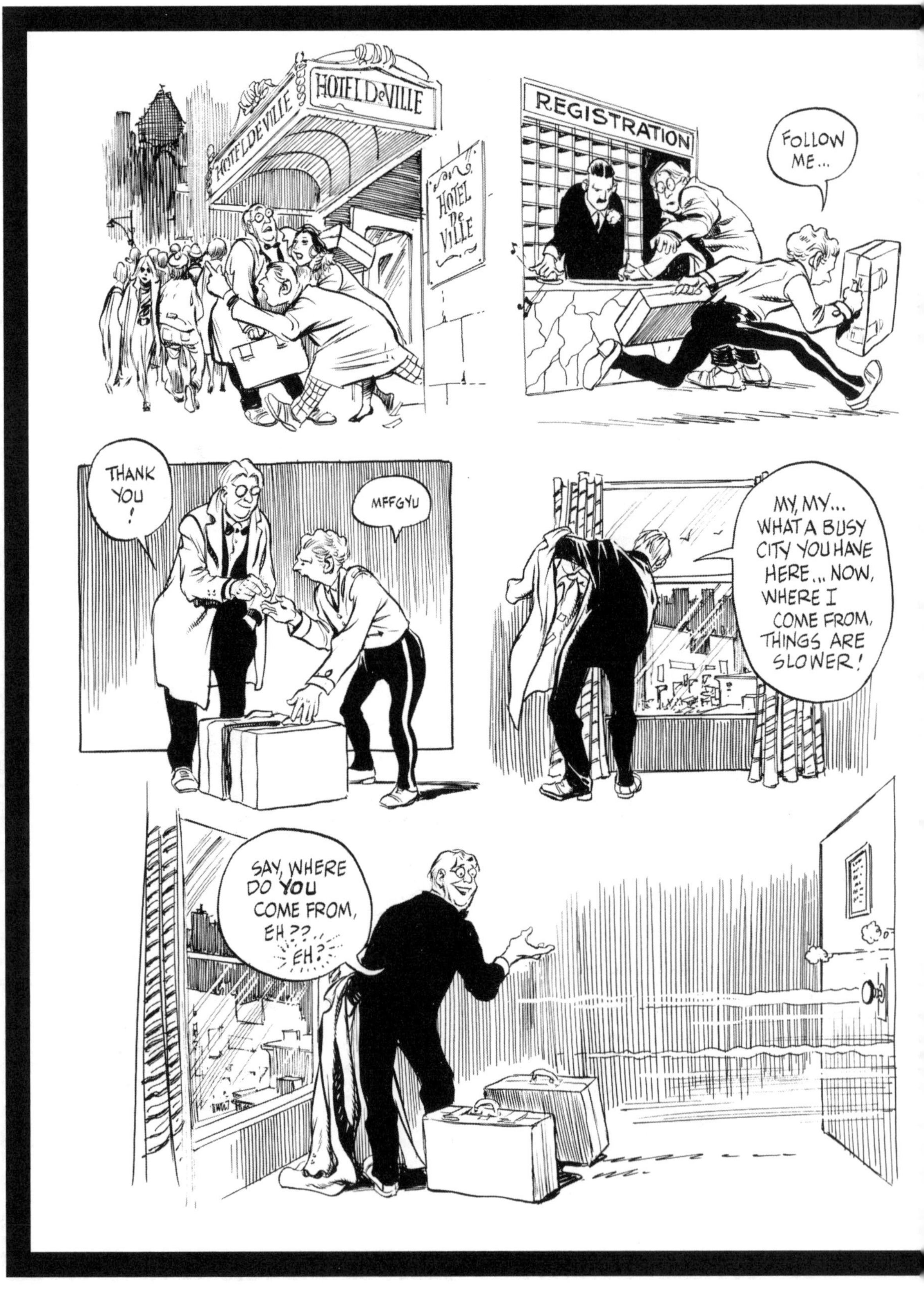
HOTEL DeVILLE
HOTEL DeVILLE
HOTEL De VILLE
REGISTRATION
FOLLOW ME...
THANK YOU!
MFFGYU
MY, MY... WHAT A BUSY CITY YOU HAVE HERE... NOW, WHERE I COME FROM, THINGS ARE SLOWER!
SAY, WHERE DO YOU COME FROM, EH??
EH?

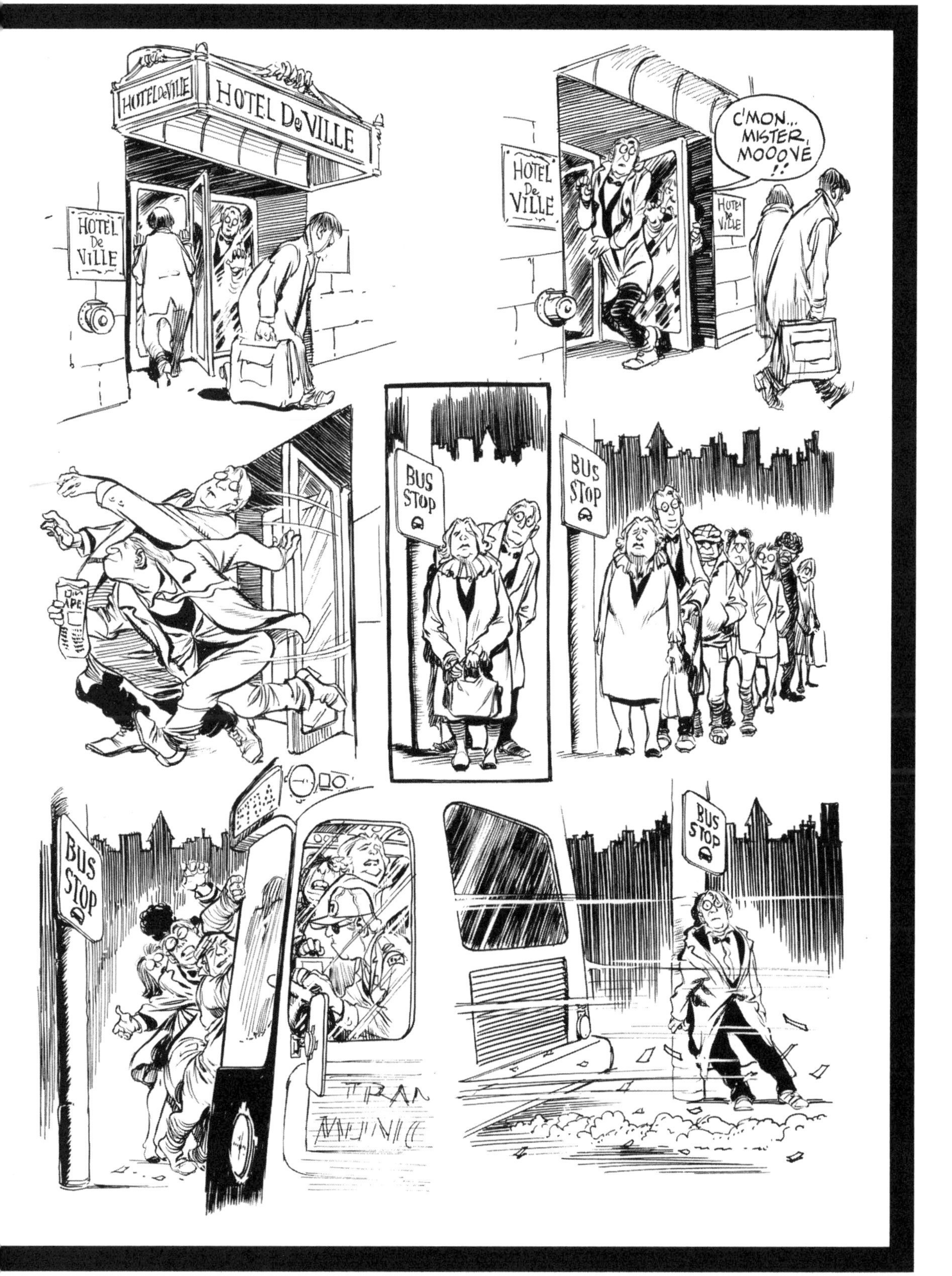
HOTEL DeVILLE
HOTEL DeVILLE
HOTEL De VILLE
HOTEL De VILLE
C'MON... MISTER, MOOOVE!!
BUS STOP
BUS STOP
BUS STOP
BUS STOP
BUS STOP

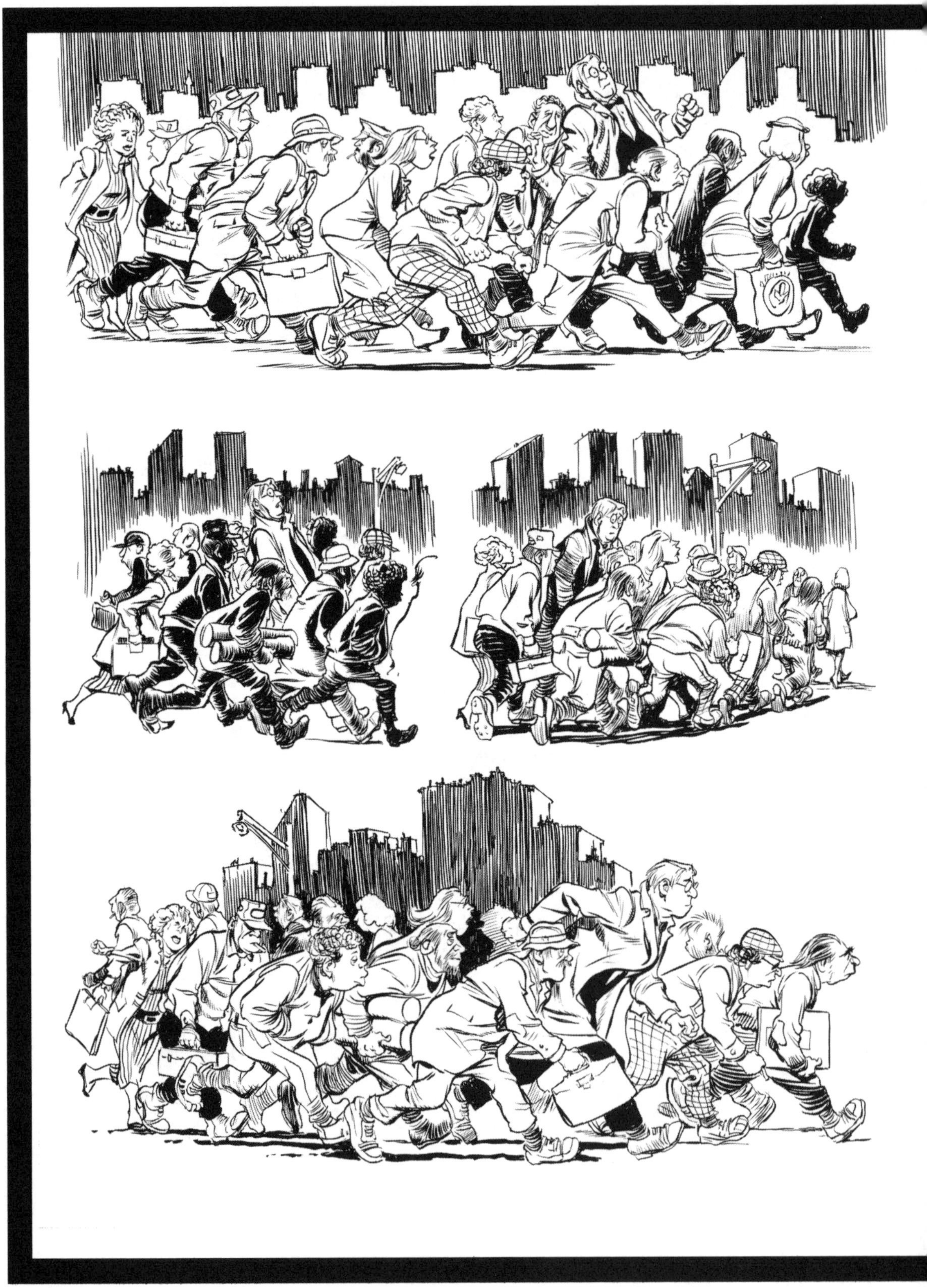

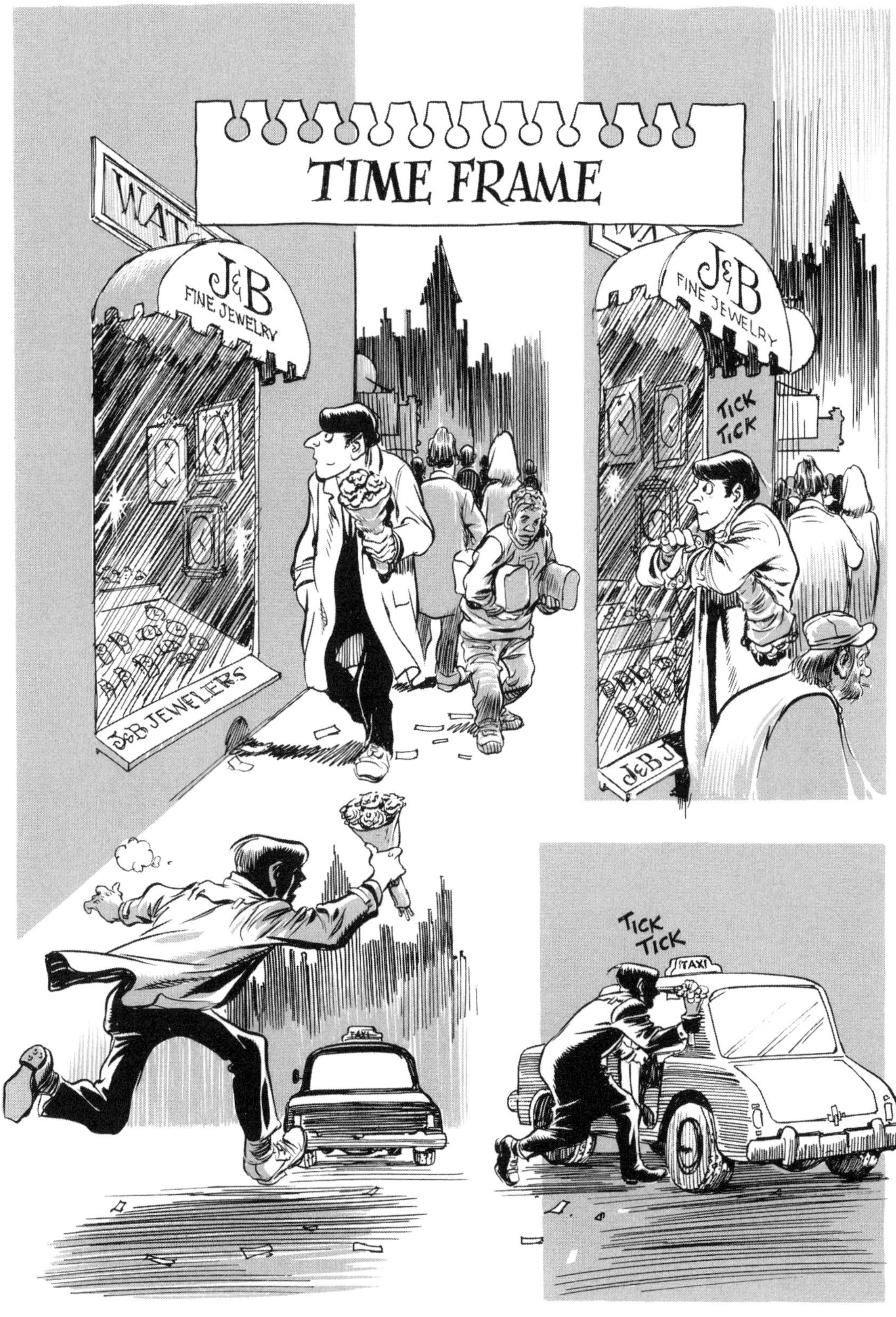
TIME FRAME
WAT
J&B FINE JEWELRY
J&B JEWELERS
J&B FINE JEWELRY
TICK
TICK
J&B J
TICK
TICK
TAXI
TAXI

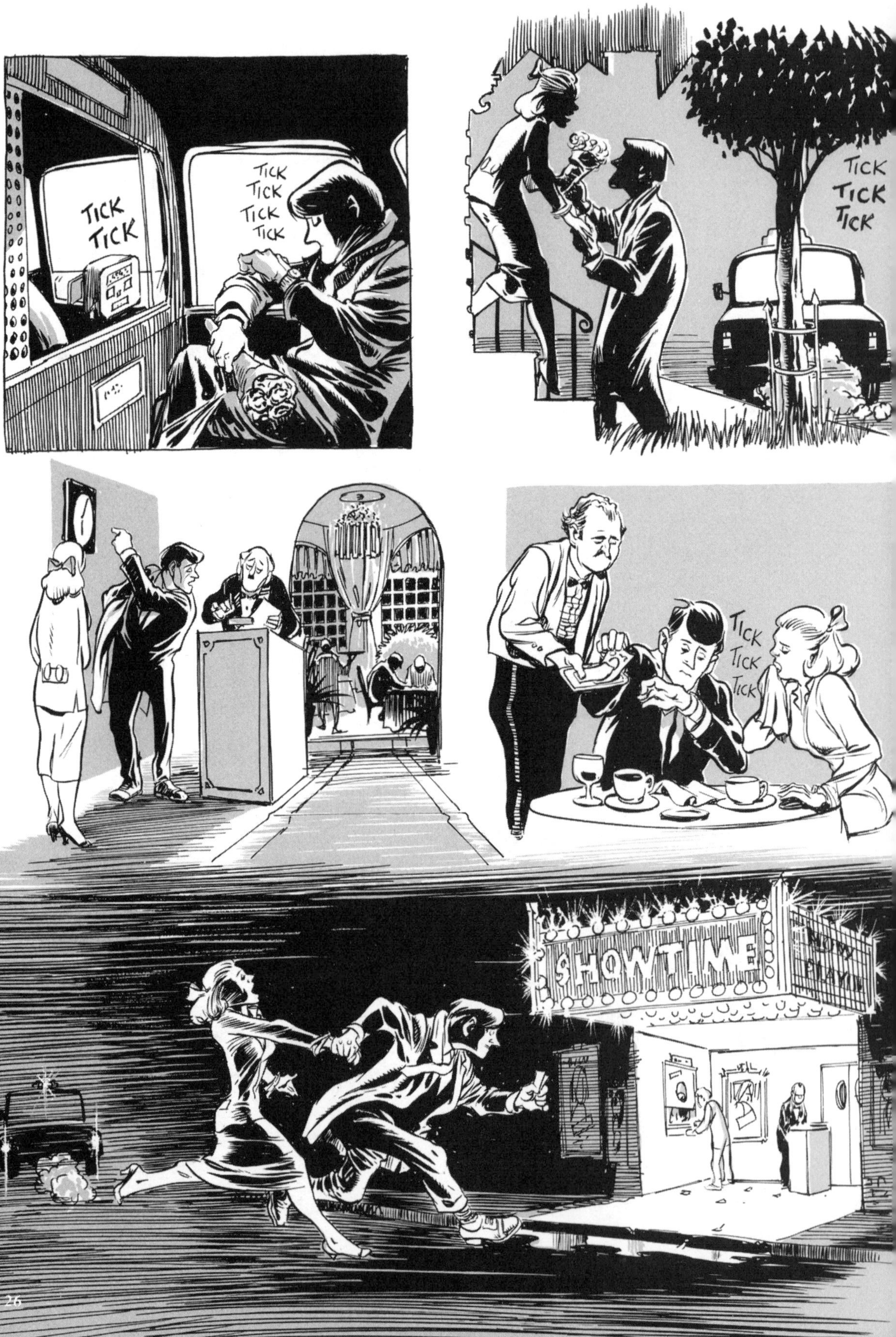

TICK
TICK
TICK
TICK
TICK
TICK
TICK
TICK
TICK
TICK
TICK
TICK
TICK
SHOWTIME

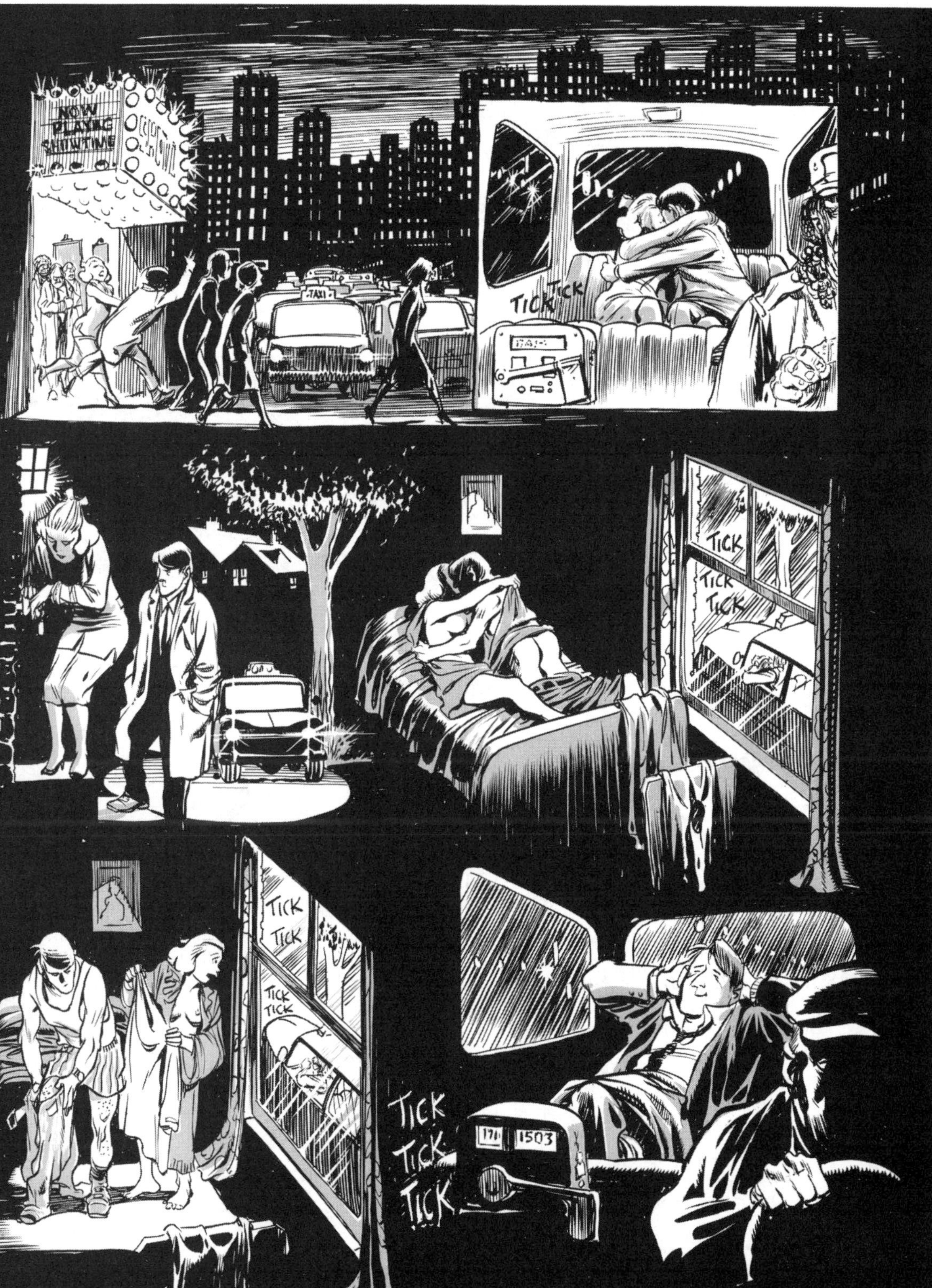
NOW PLAYING SHOWTIME
TAXI
TICK TICK
TICK
TICK TICK
TICK TICK
TICK TICK
TICK TICK TICK
171 1503

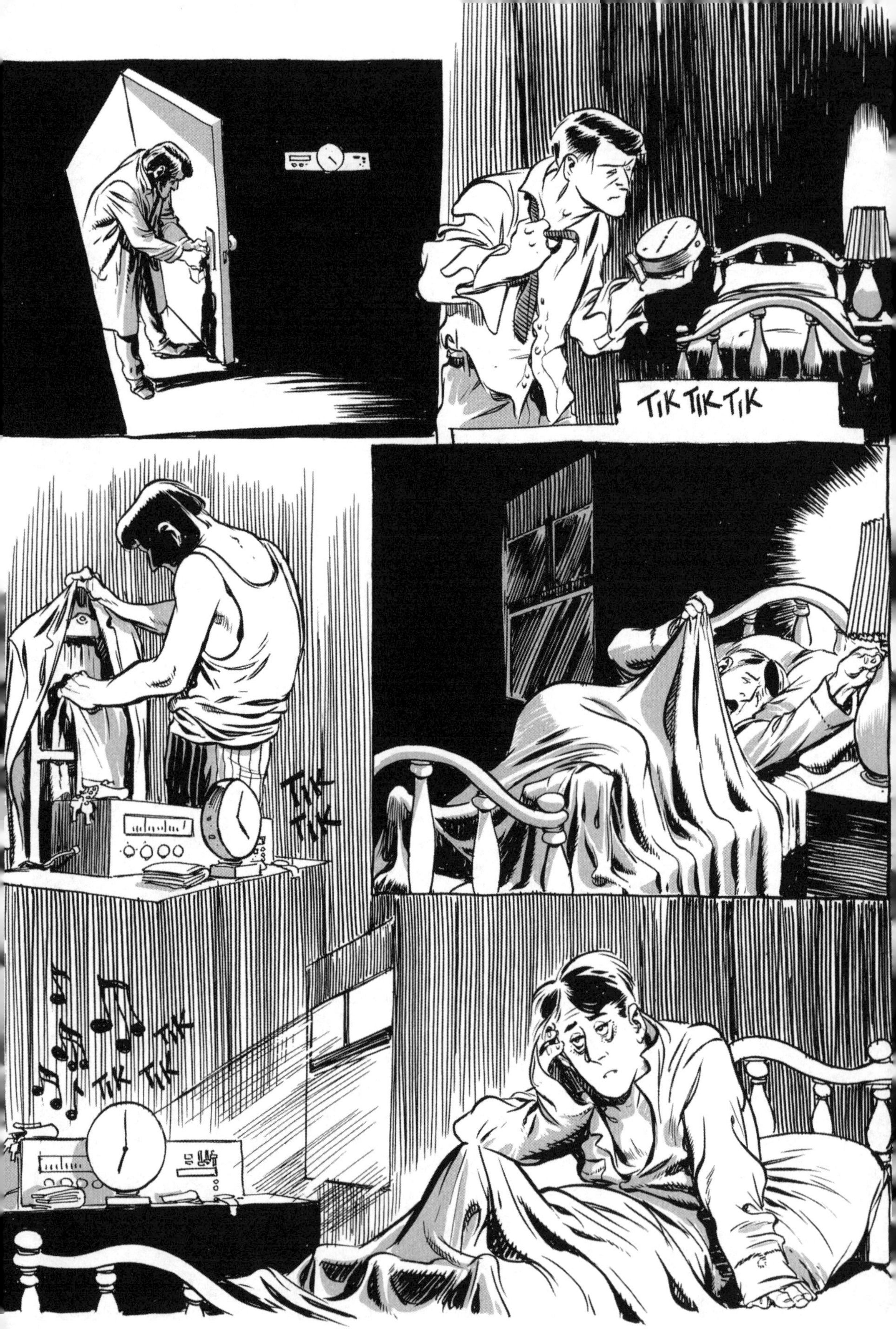
TIK TIK TIK
TIK
TIK
TIK
TIK
TIK

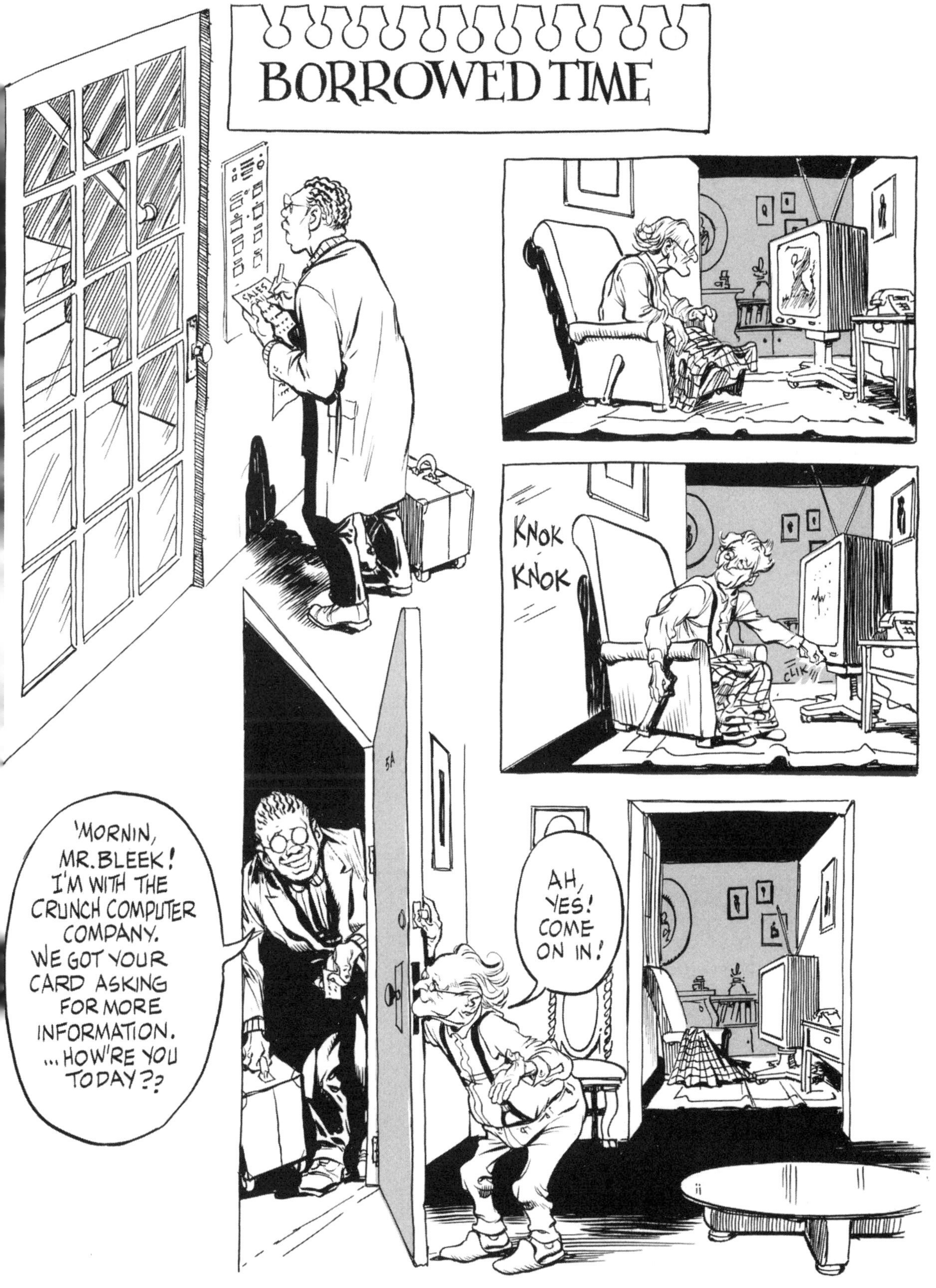
BORROWED TIME
KNOK KNOK
CLIK
'MORNIN, MR. BLEEK! I'M WITH THE CRUNCH COMPUTER COMPANY. WE GOT YOUR CARD ASKING FOR MORE INFORMATION. ...HOW'RE YOU TODAY??
AH, YES! COME ON IN!

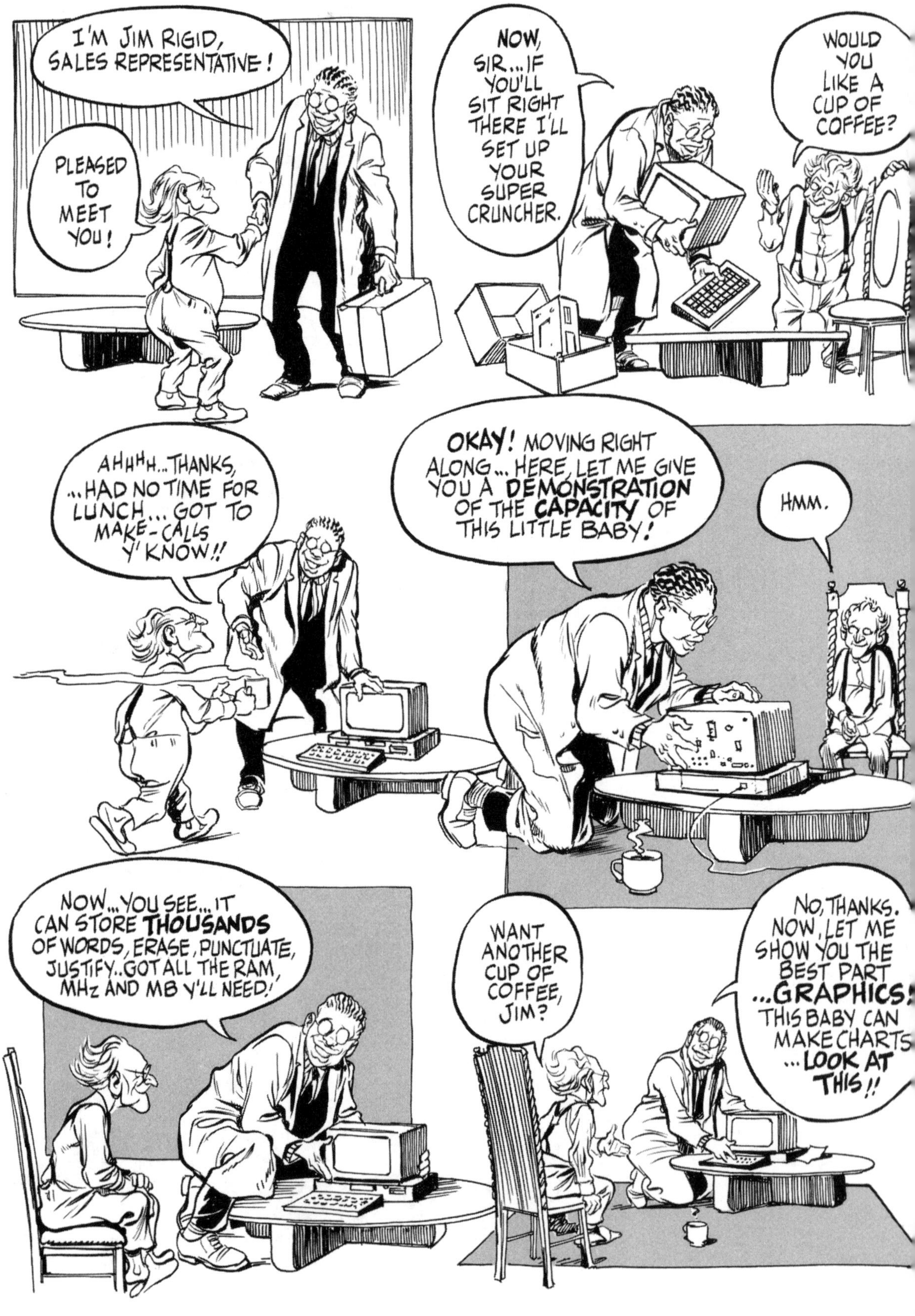
I'M JIM RIGID, SALES REPRESENTATIVE!
PLEASED TO MEET YOU!
NOW, SIR... IF YOU'LL SIT RIGHT THERE I'LL SET UP YOUR SUPER CRUNCHER.
WOULD YOU LIKE A CUP OF COFFEE?
AHHHH... THANKS, ...HAD NO TIME FOR LUNCH... GOT TO MAKE-CALLS Y'KNOW!!
OKAY! MOVING RIGHT ALONG... HERE, LET ME GIVE YOU A DEMONSTRATION OF THE CAPACITY OF THIS LITTLE BABY!
HMM.
NOW... YOU SEE... IT CAN STORE THOUSANDS OF WORDS, ERASE, PUNCTUATE, JUSTIFY.. GOT ALL THE RAM, MHz AND MB Y'LL NEED!
WANT ANOTHER CUP OF COFFEE, JIM?
NO, THANKS. NOW, LET ME SHOW YOU THE BEST PART ...GRAPHICS! THIS BABY CAN MAKE CHARTS ...LOOK AT THIS!!

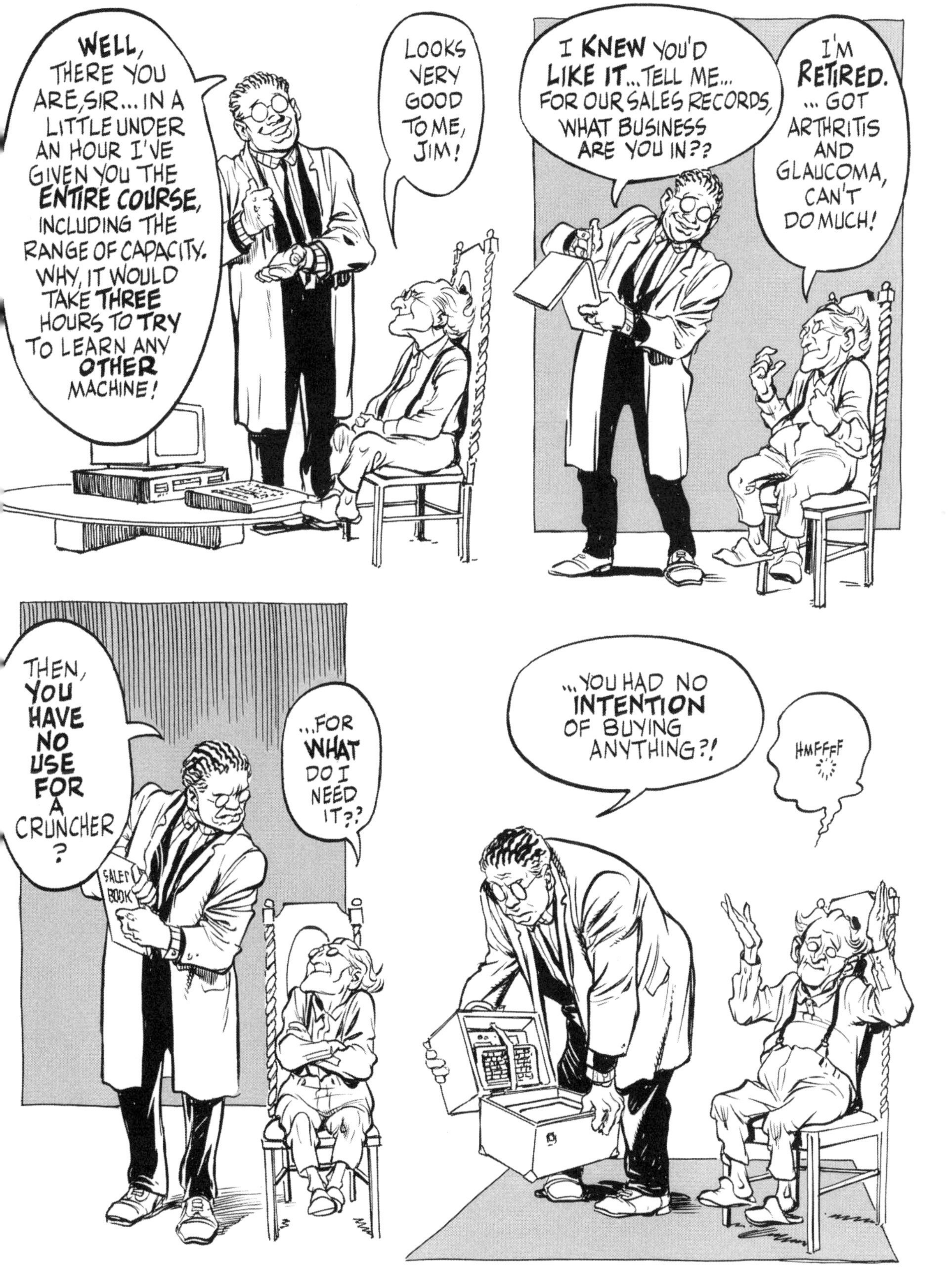
WELL, THERE YOU ARE, SIR... IN A LITTLE UNDER AN HOUR I'VE GIVEN YOU THE ENTIRE COURSE, INCLUDING THE RANGE OF CAPACITY. WHY, IT WOULD TAKE THREE HOURS TO TRY TO LEARN ANY OTHER MACHINE!
LOOKS VERY GOOD TO ME, JIM!
I KNEW YOU'D LIKE IT... TELL ME... FOR OUR SALES RECORDS, WHAT BUSINESS ARE YOU IN??
I'M RETIRED. ... GOT ARTHRITIS AND GLAUCOMA, CAN'T DO MUCH!
THEN, YOU HAVE NO USE FOR A CRUNCHER?
...FOR WHAT DO I NEED IT??
SALES BOOK
...YOU HAD NO INTENTION OF BUYING ANYTHING?!
HMFFFF

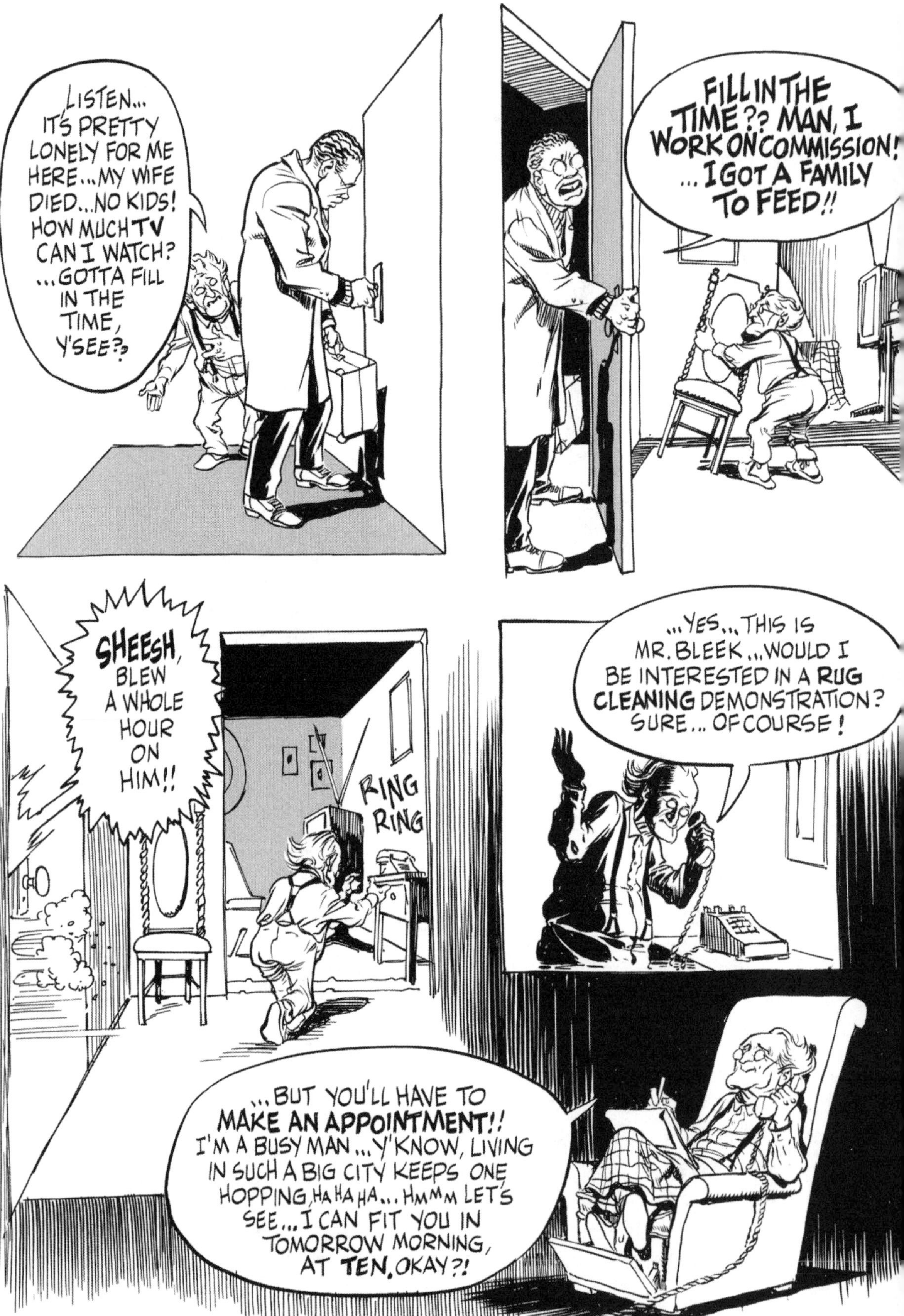
LISTEN... IT'S PRETTY LONELY FOR ME HERE...MY WIFE DIED...NO KIDS! HOW MUCH TV CAN I WATCH? ...GOTTA FILL IN THE TIME, Y'SEE?
FILL IN THE TIME?? MAN, I WORK ON COMMISSION! ...I GOT A FAMILY TO FEED!!
SHEESH, BLEW A WHOLE HOUR ON HIM!!
RING RING
...YES... THIS IS MR. BLEEK... WOULD I BE INTERESTED IN A RUG CLEANING DEMONSTRATION? SURE... OF COURSE!
...BUT YOU'LL HAVE TO MAKE AN APPOINTMENT!! I'M A BUSY MAN... Y'KNOW, LIVING IN SUCH A BIG CITY KEEPS ONE HOPPING, HA HA HA... HMMM LET'S SEE... I CAN FIT YOU IN TOMORROW MORNING, AT TEN, OKAY?!

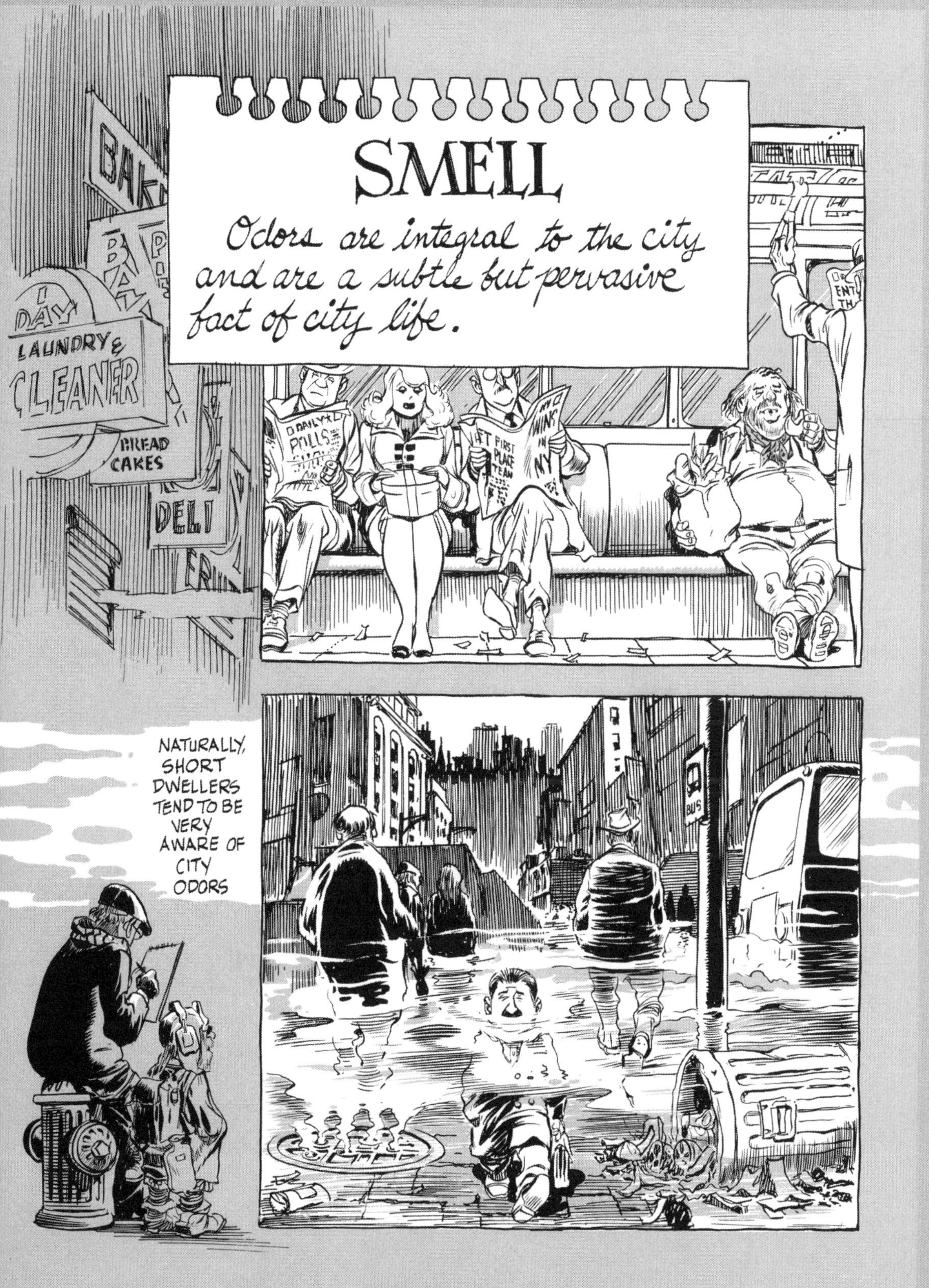
SMELL
Odors are integral to the city and are a subtle but pervasive fact of city life.
1 DAY
LAUNDRY &
CLEANER
BREAD
CAKES
DELI
NATURALLY, SHORT DWELLERS TEND TO BE VERY AWARE OF CITY ODORS
BUS

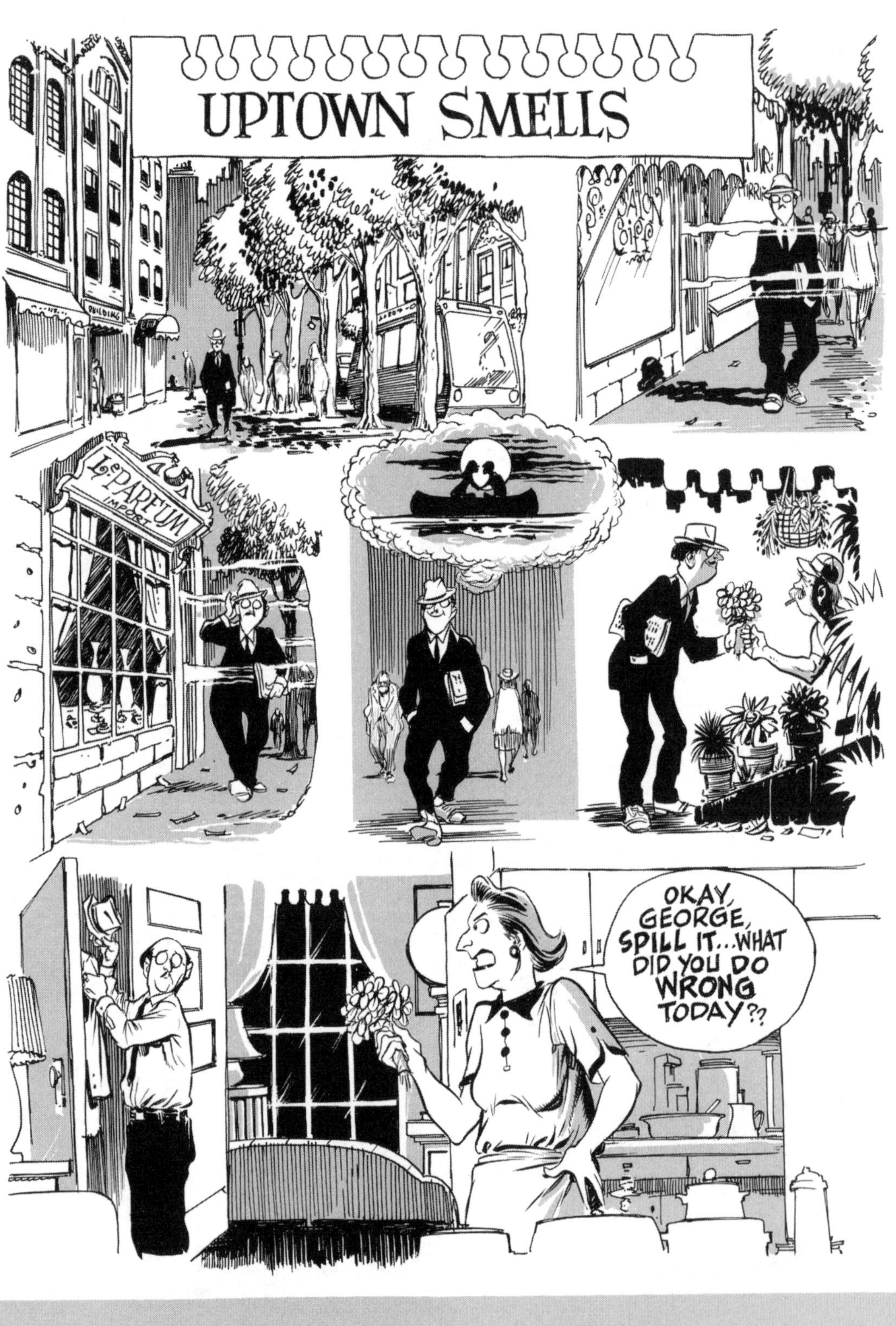
UPTOWN SMELLS
Le PARFUM IMPORT
OKAY, GEORGE, SPILL IT...WHAT DID YOU DO WRONG TODAY??

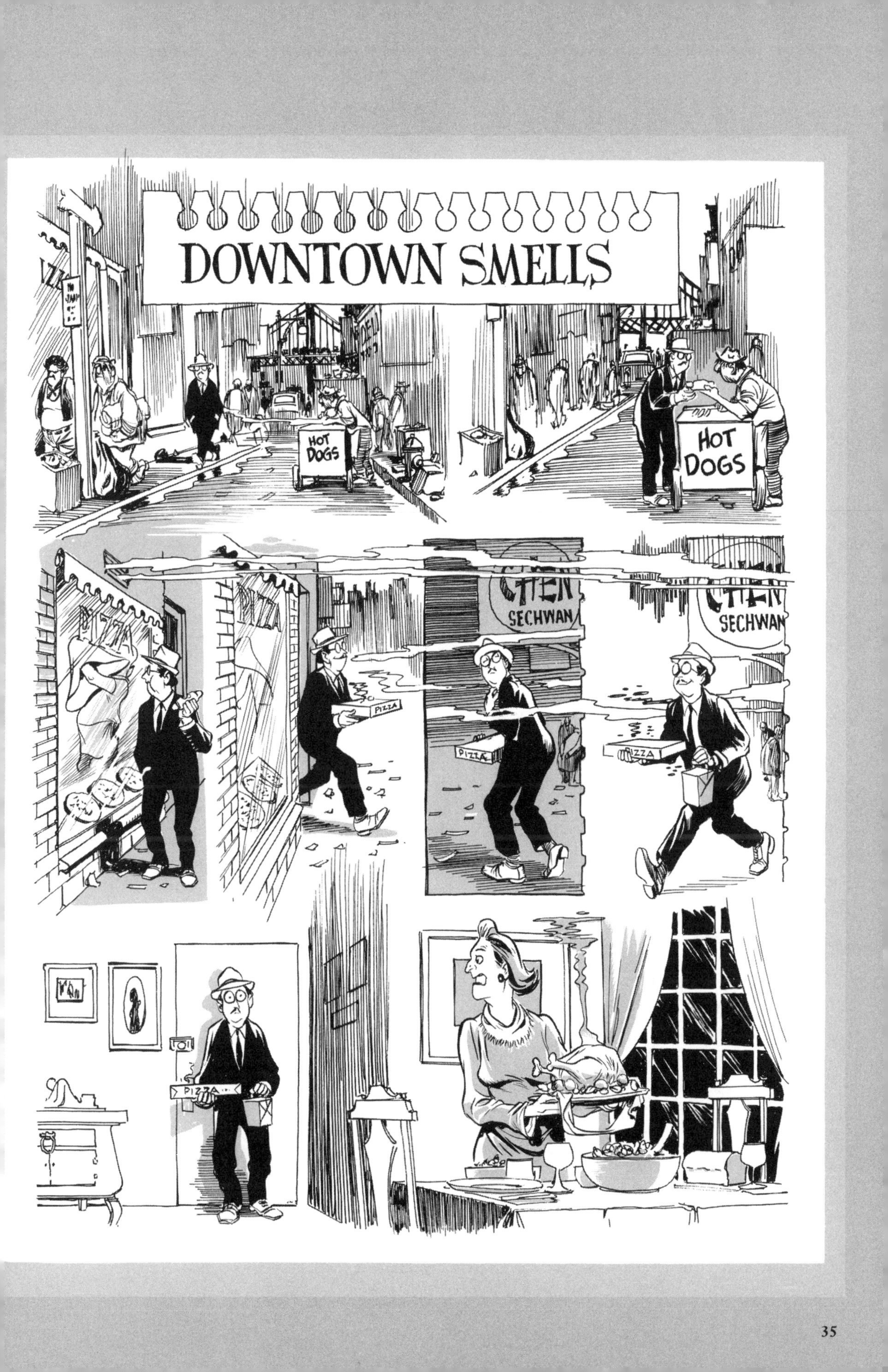
DOWNTOWN SMELLS
HOT DOGS
HOT DOGS
PIZZA
PIZZA
SECHWAN
PIZZA
PIZZA
SECHWAN
PIZZA
PIZZA

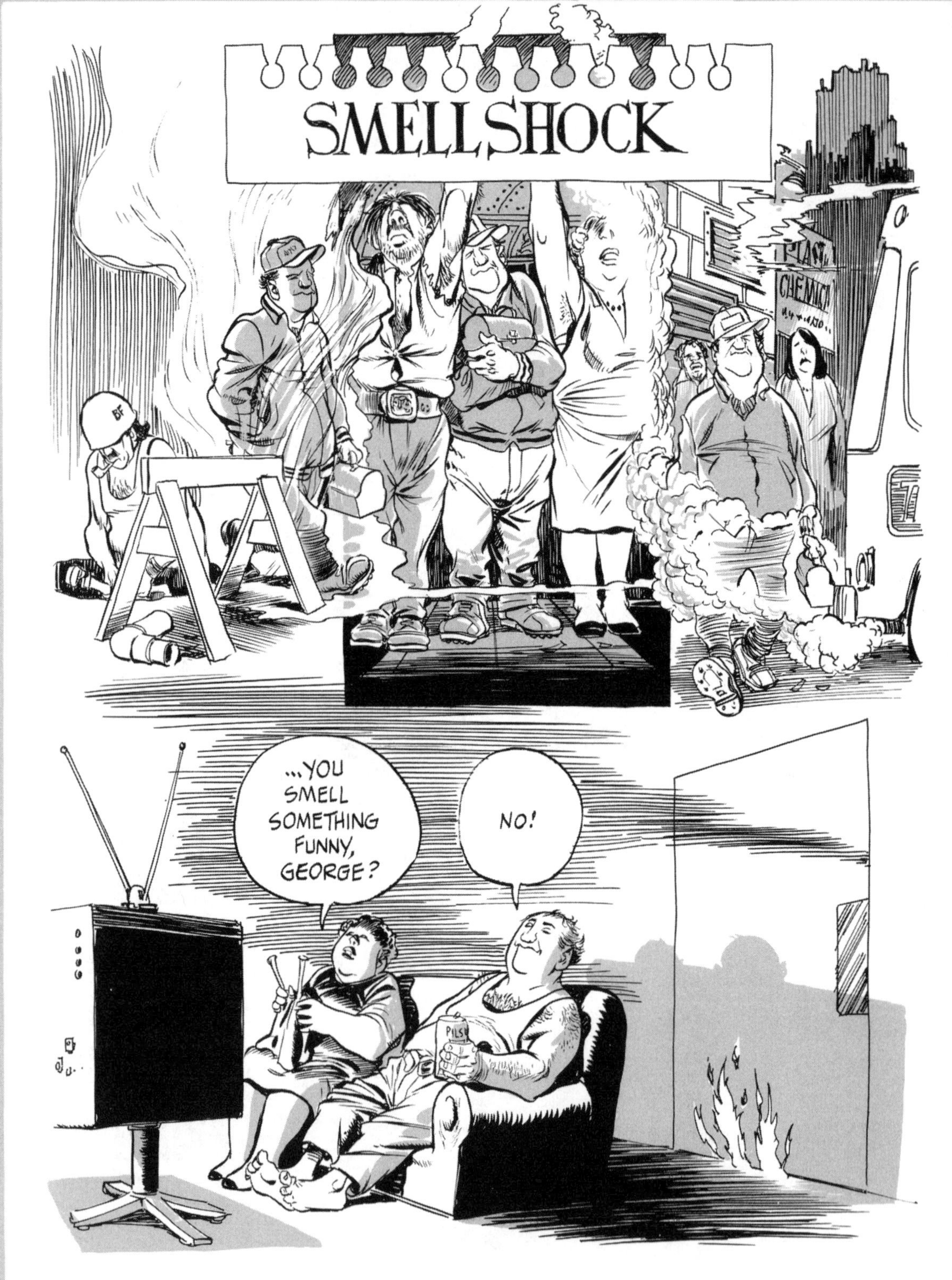
SMELLSHOCK
...YOU SMELL SOMETHING FUNNY, GEORGE?
NO!

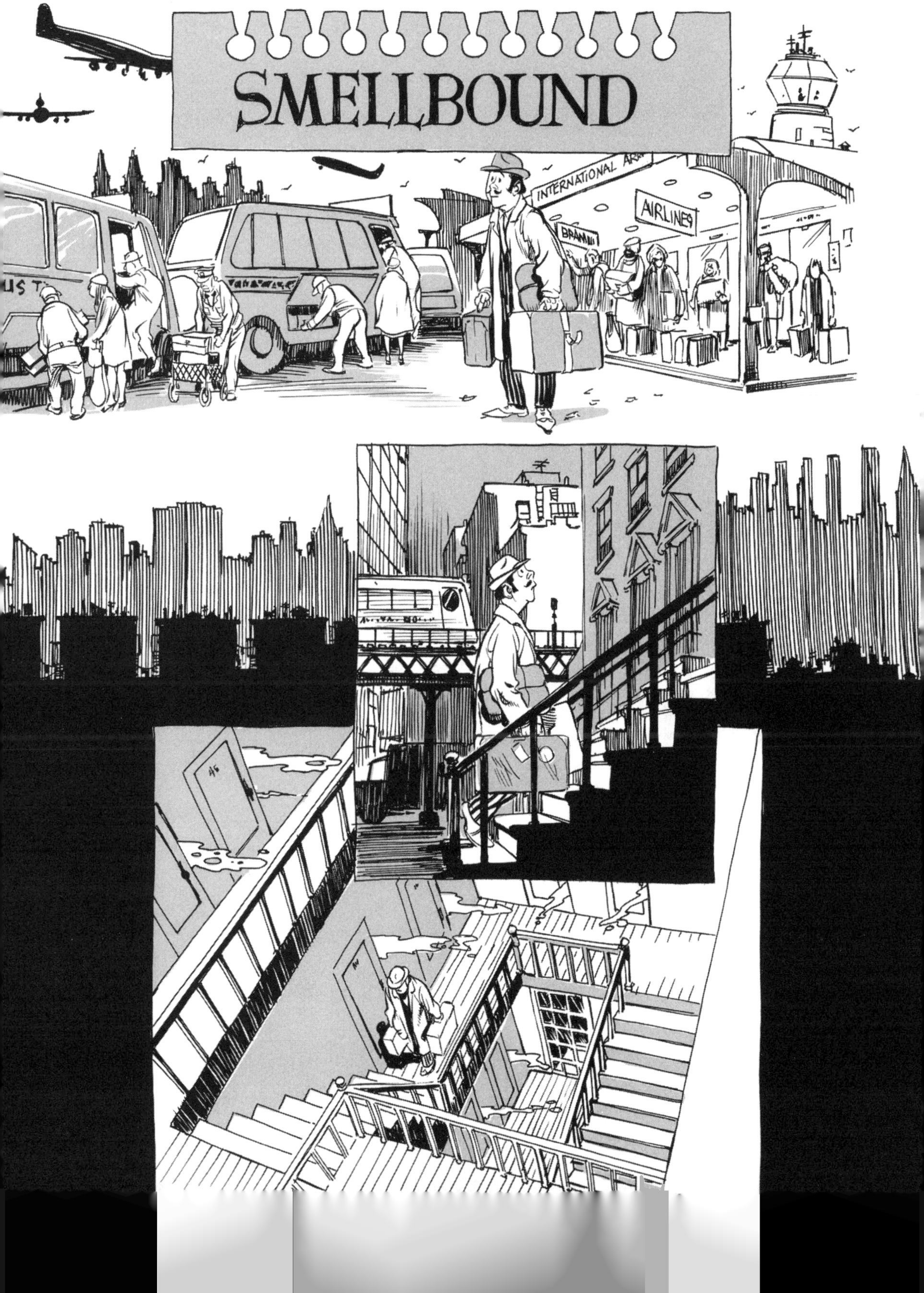
SMELLBOUND
INTERNATIONAL
AIRLINES

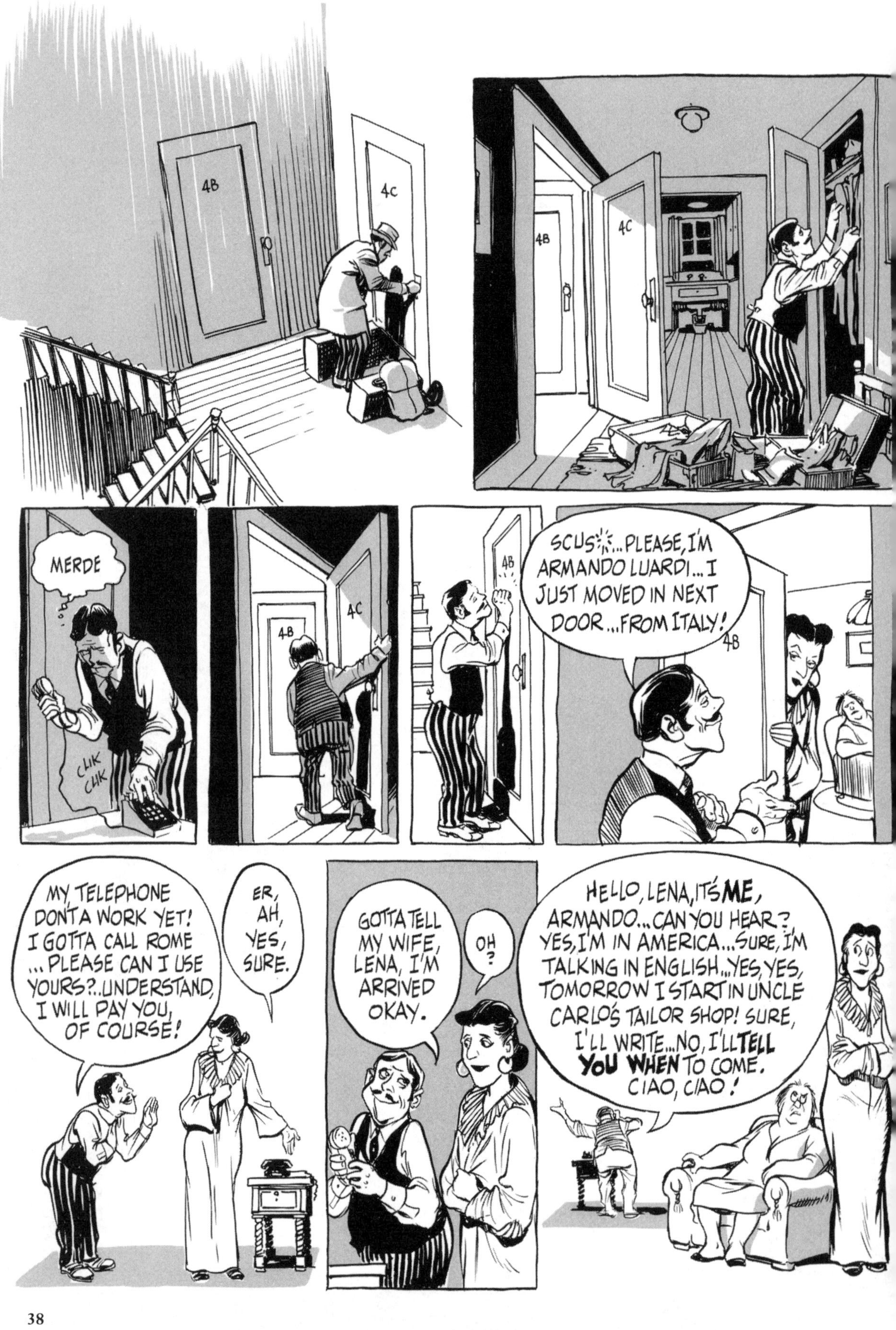
4B
4C
4B
4C
MERDE
CLIK CLIK
4B
4C
4B
SCUS... PLEASE, I'M ARMANDO LUARDI... I JUST MOVED IN NEXT DOOR... FROM ITALY!
4B
MY TELEPHONE DON'TA WORK YET! I GOTTA CALL ROME ... PLEASE CAN I USE YOURS?..UNDERSTAND, I WILL PAY YOU, OF COURSE!
ER, AH, YES, SURE.
GOTTA TELL MY WIFE, LENA, I'M ARRIVED OKAY.
OH?
HELLO, LENA, IT'S **ME**, ARMANDO... CAN YOU HEAR? YES, I'M IN AMERICA... SURE, I'M TALKING IN ENGLISH... YES, YES, TOMORROW I START IN UNCLE CARLO'S TAILOR SHOP! SURE, I'LL WRITE... NO, I'LL **TELL YOU WHEN** TO COME. CIAO, CIAO!

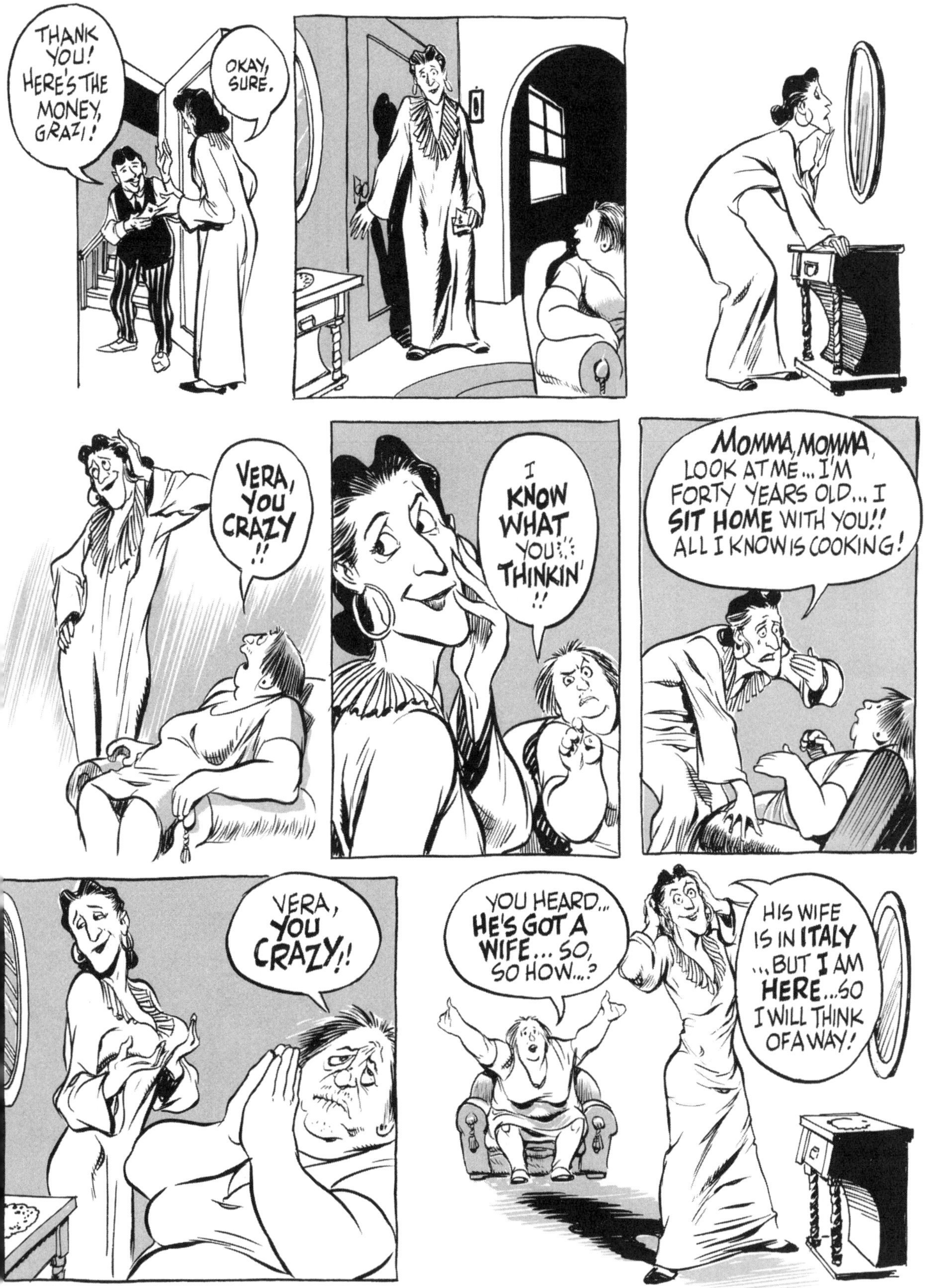
THANK YOU! HERE'S THE MONEY, GRAZI!
OKAY, SURE.
VERA, YOU CRAZY!!
I KNOW WHAT YOU THINKIN'!!
MOMMA, MOMMA, LOOK AT ME... I'M FORTY YEARS OLD... I SIT HOME WITH YOU!! ALL I KNOW IS COOKING!
VERA, YOU CRAZY!!
YOU HEARD... HE'S GOT A WIFE... SO, SO HOW...?
HIS WIFE IS IN ITALY ...BUT I AM HERE...SO I WILL THINK OF A WAY!

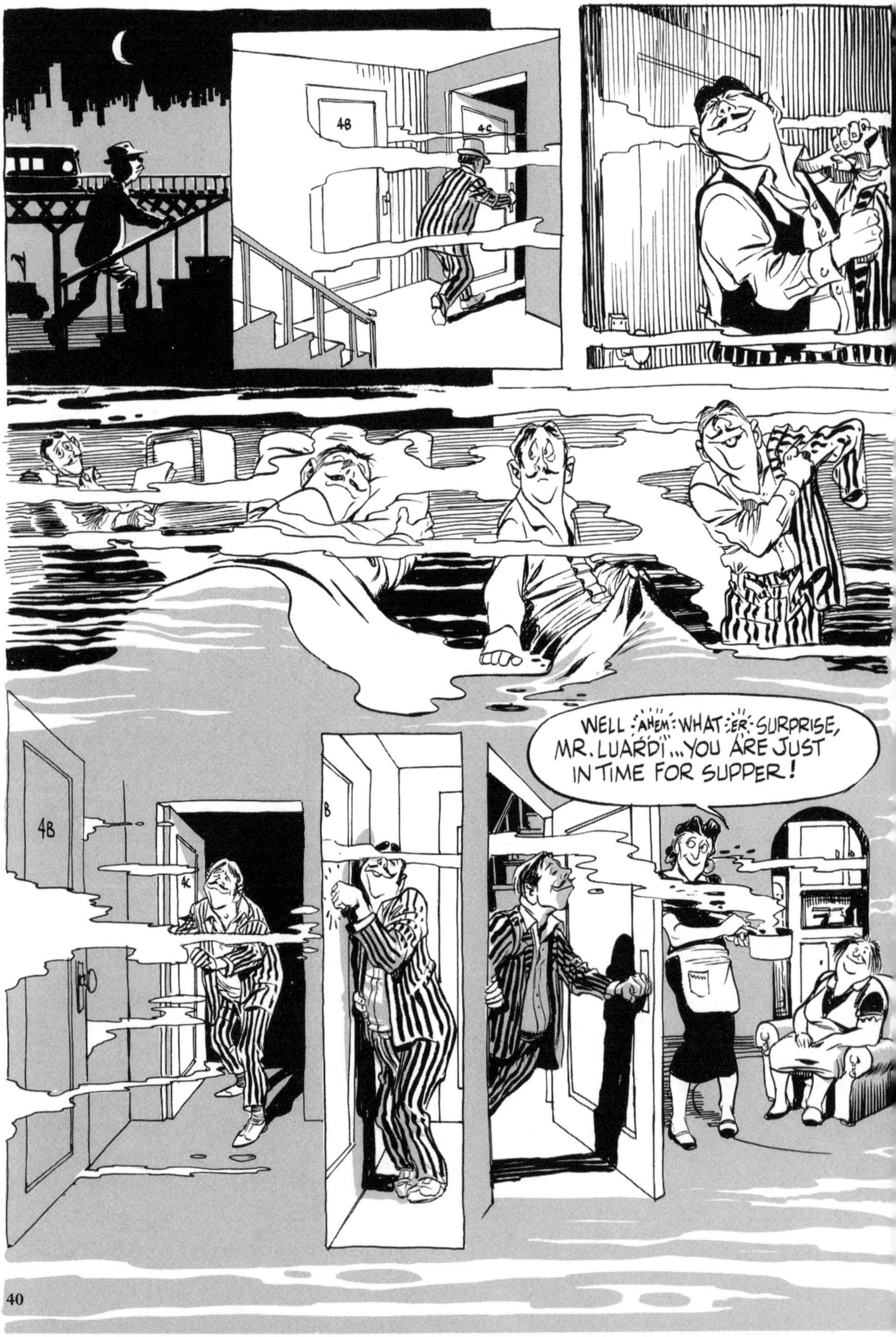
4B
4C
4B
4C
B
WELL AHEM WHAT ER SURPRISE, MR. LUARDI... YOU ARE JUST IN TIME FOR SUPPER!

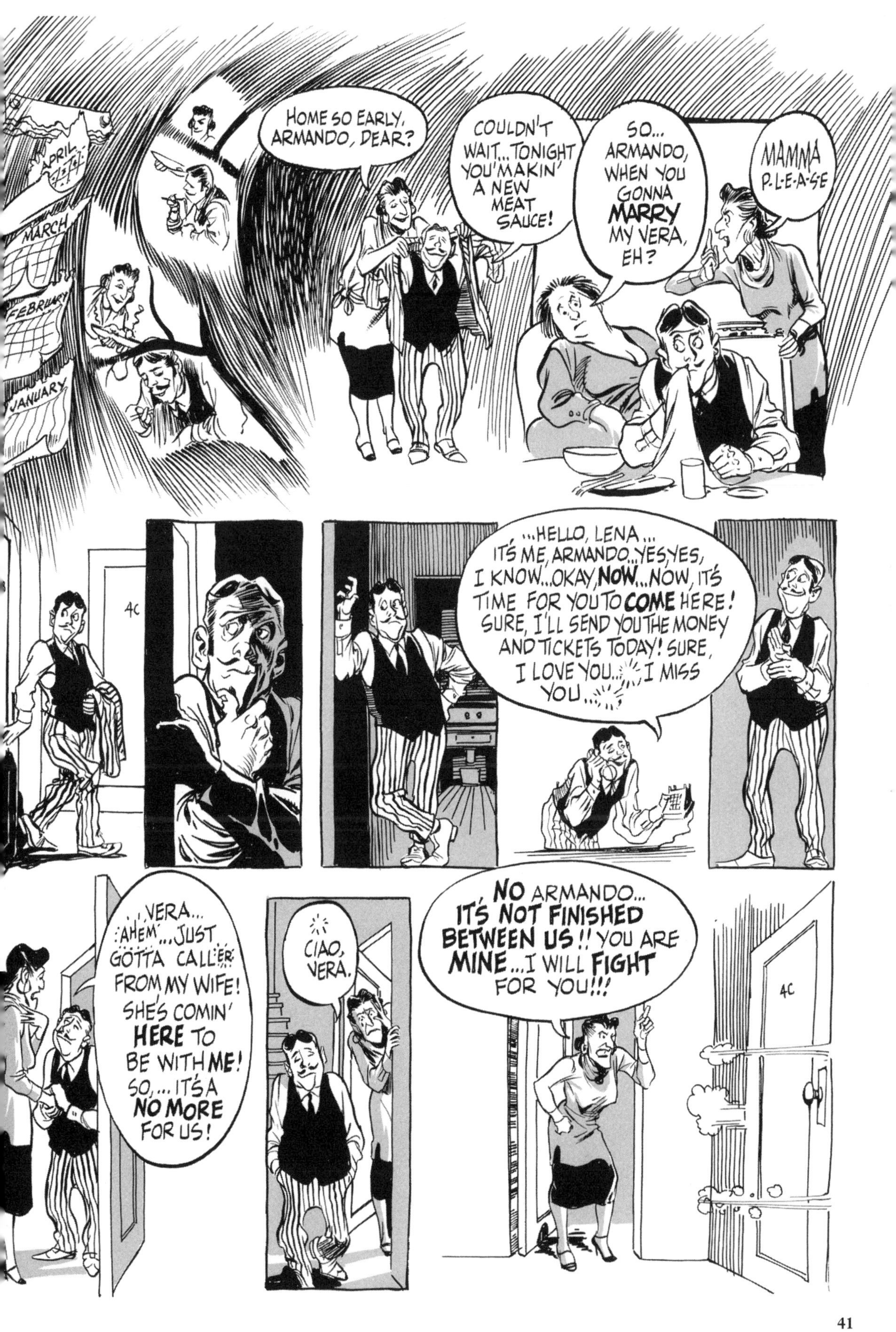

APRIL
MARCH
FEBRUARY
JANUARY
HOME SO EARLY, ARMANDO, DEAR?
COULDN'T WAIT... TONIGHT YOU'MAKIN' A NEW MEAT SAUCE!
SO... ARMANDO, WHEN YOU GONNA MARRY MY VERA, EH?
MAMMA P-L-E-A-SE
4C
...HELLO, LENA... IT'S ME, ARMANDO...YES,YES, I KNOW...OKAY, NOW...NOW, IT'S TIME FOR YOU TO COME HERE! SURE, I'LL SEND YOU THE MONEY AND TICKETS TODAY! SURE, I LOVE YOU... I MISS YOU...
...VERA... AHEM...JUST GOTTA CALL'ER FROM MY WIFE! SHE'S COMIN' HERE TO BE WITH ME! SO,...IT'S A NO MORE FOR US!
CIAO, VERA.
NO ARMANDO... IT'S NOT FINISHED BETWEEN US!! YOU ARE MINE...I WILL FIGHT FOR YOU!!!
4C

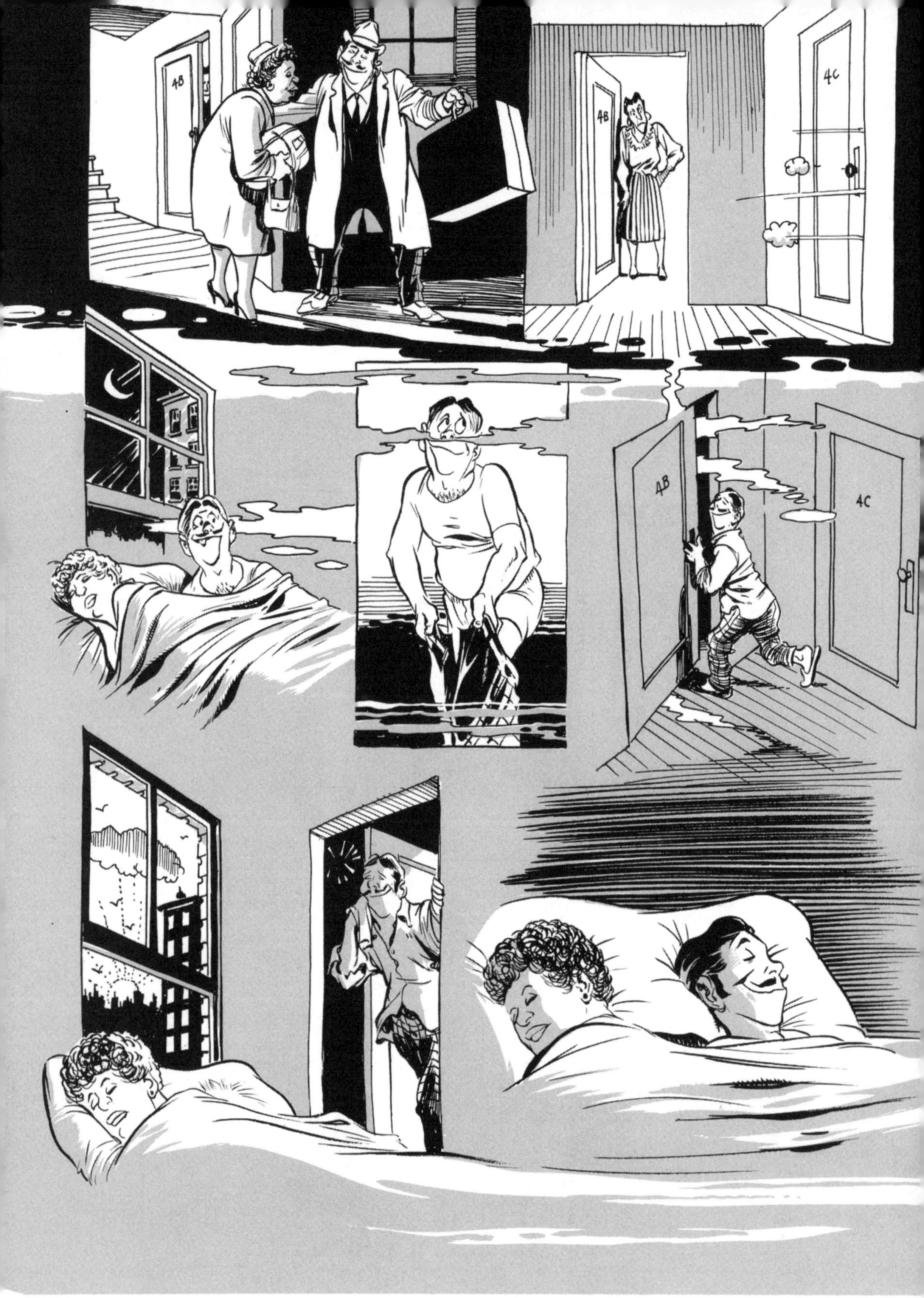
4B
4C

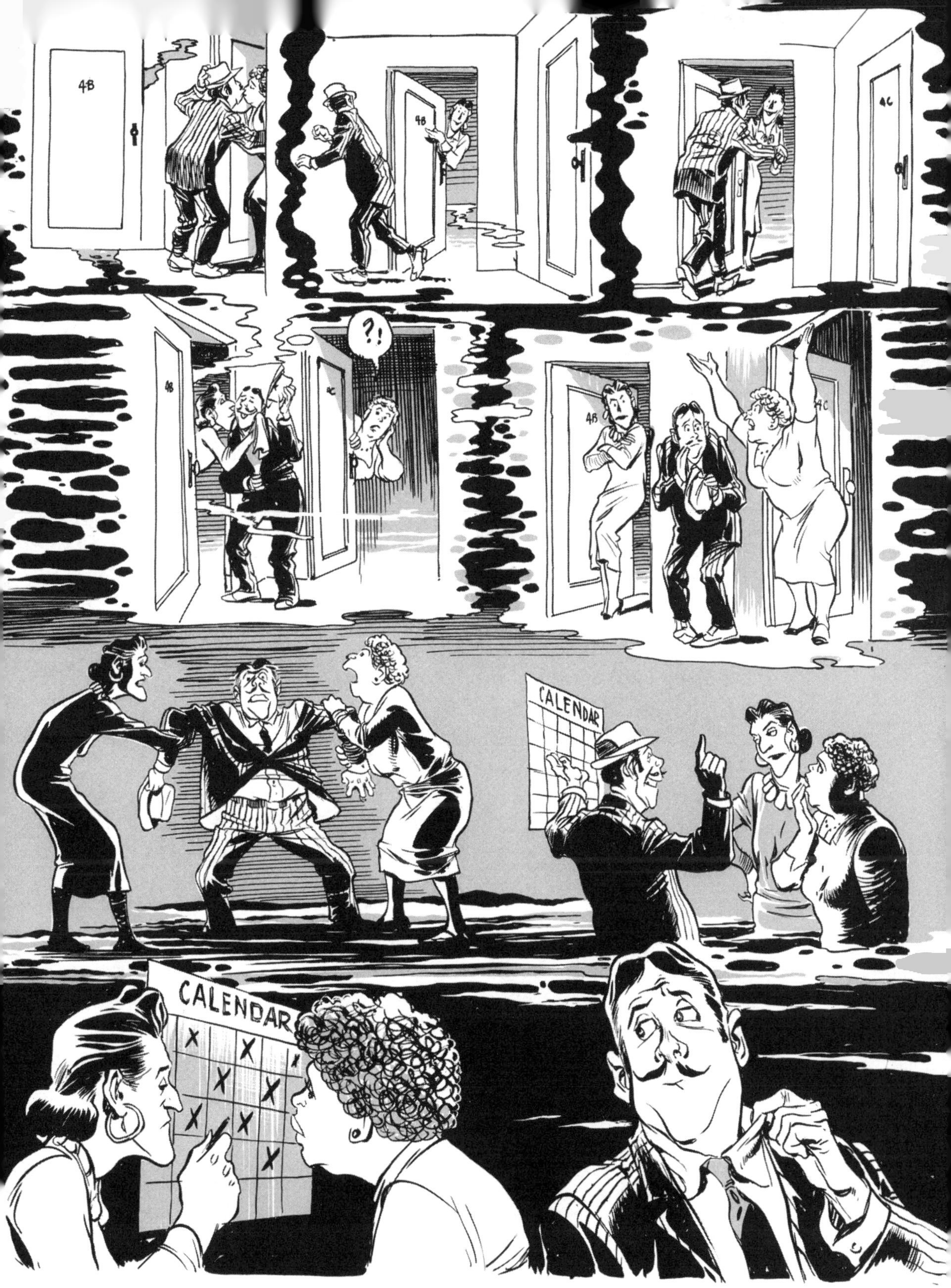
4B
4B
4C
4B
?!
4C
4B
4C
CALENDAR
CALENDAR

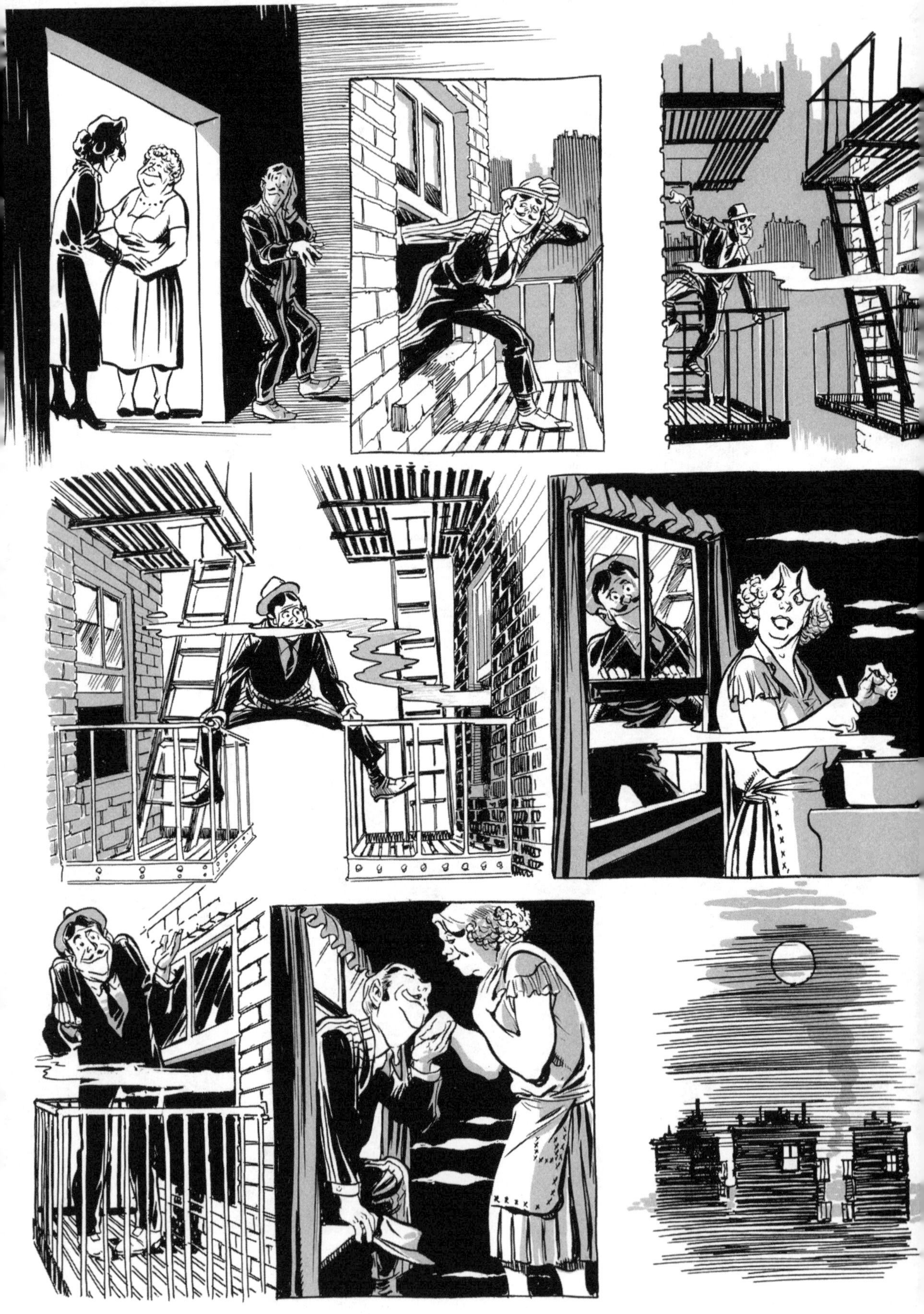

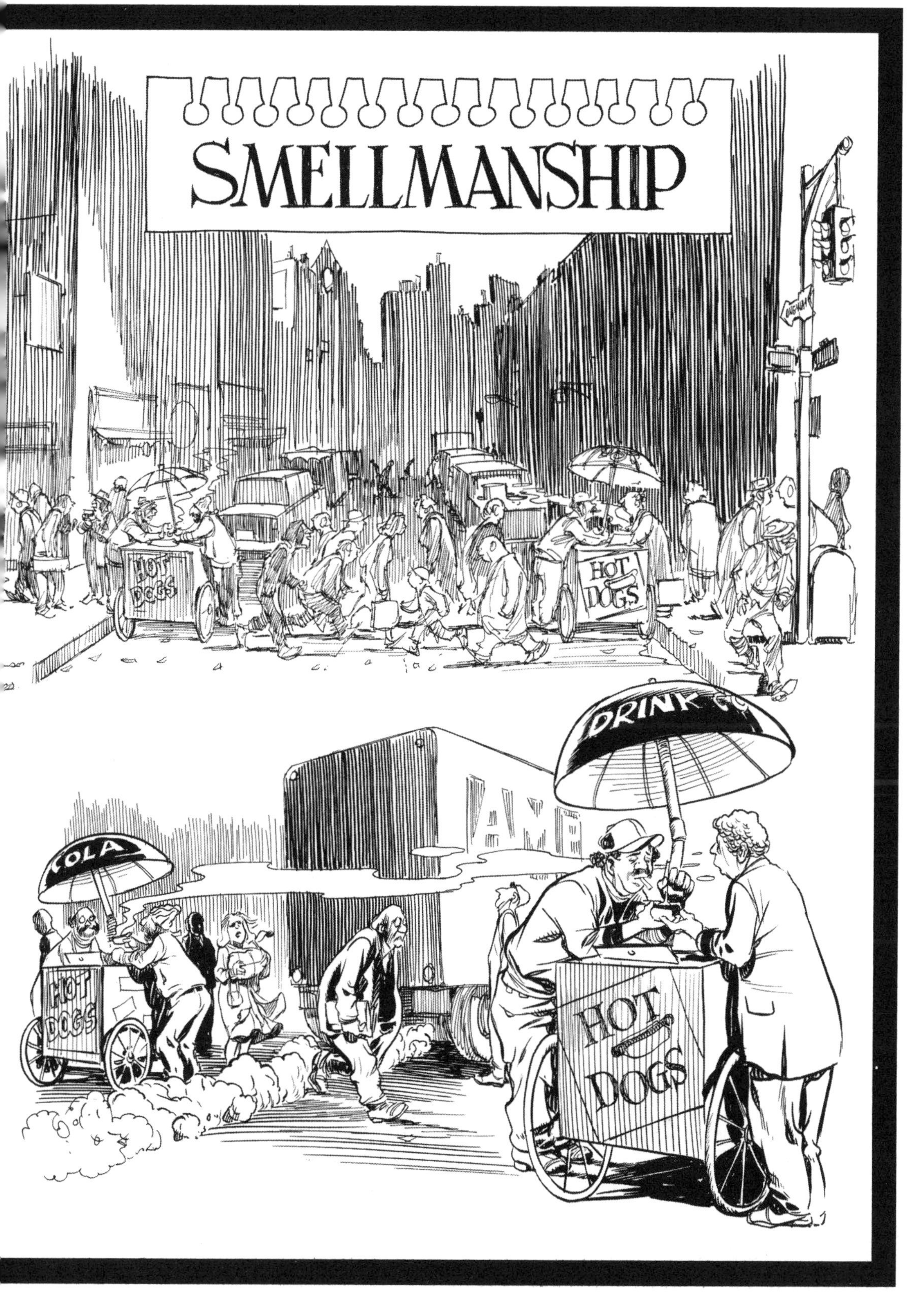
SMELLMANSHIP
HOT DOGS
HOT DOGS
DRINK
COLA
HOT DOGS
HOT DOGS

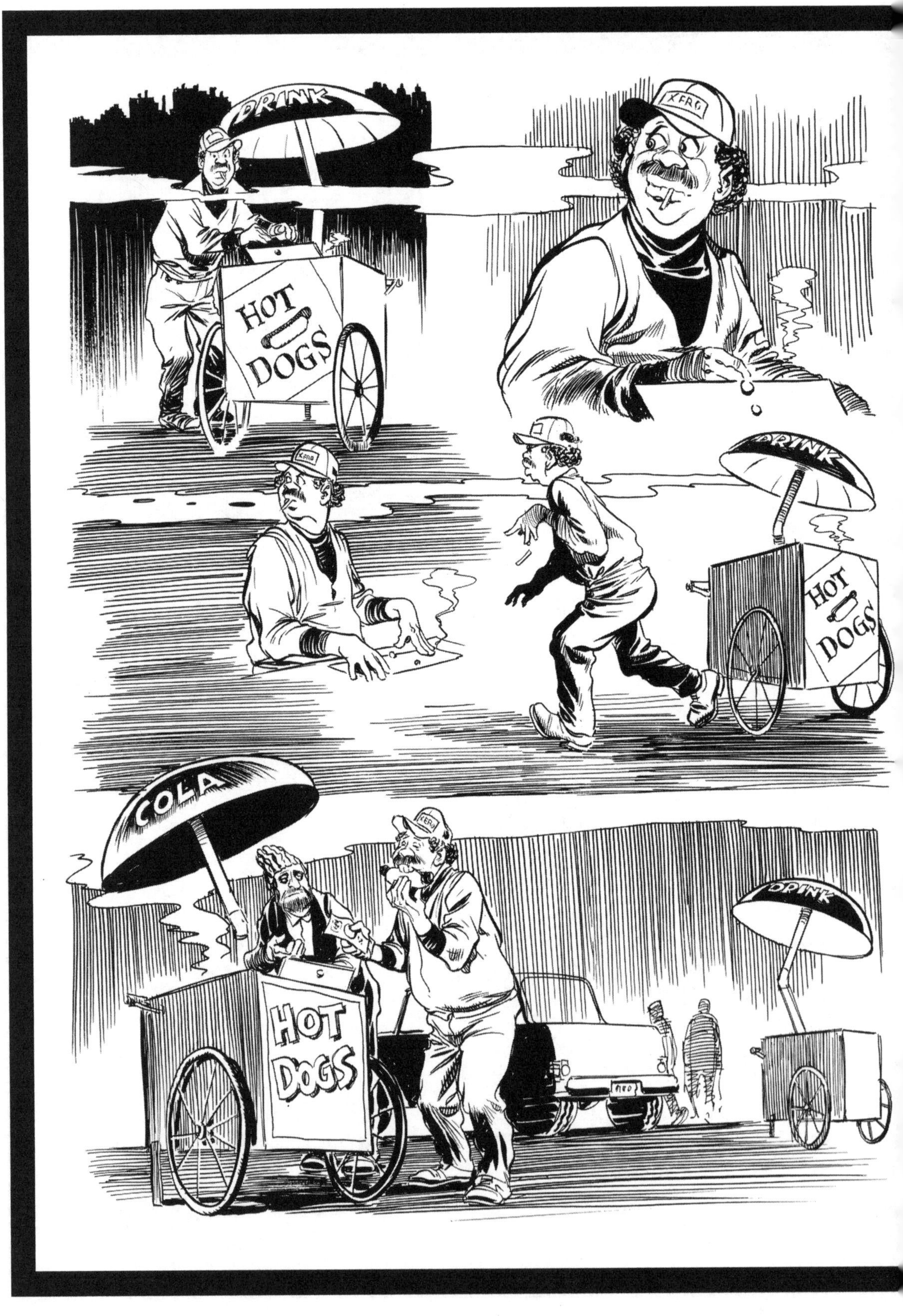
DRINK
HOT DOGS
XERO
DRINK
HOT DOGS
COLA
HOT DOGS
DRINK

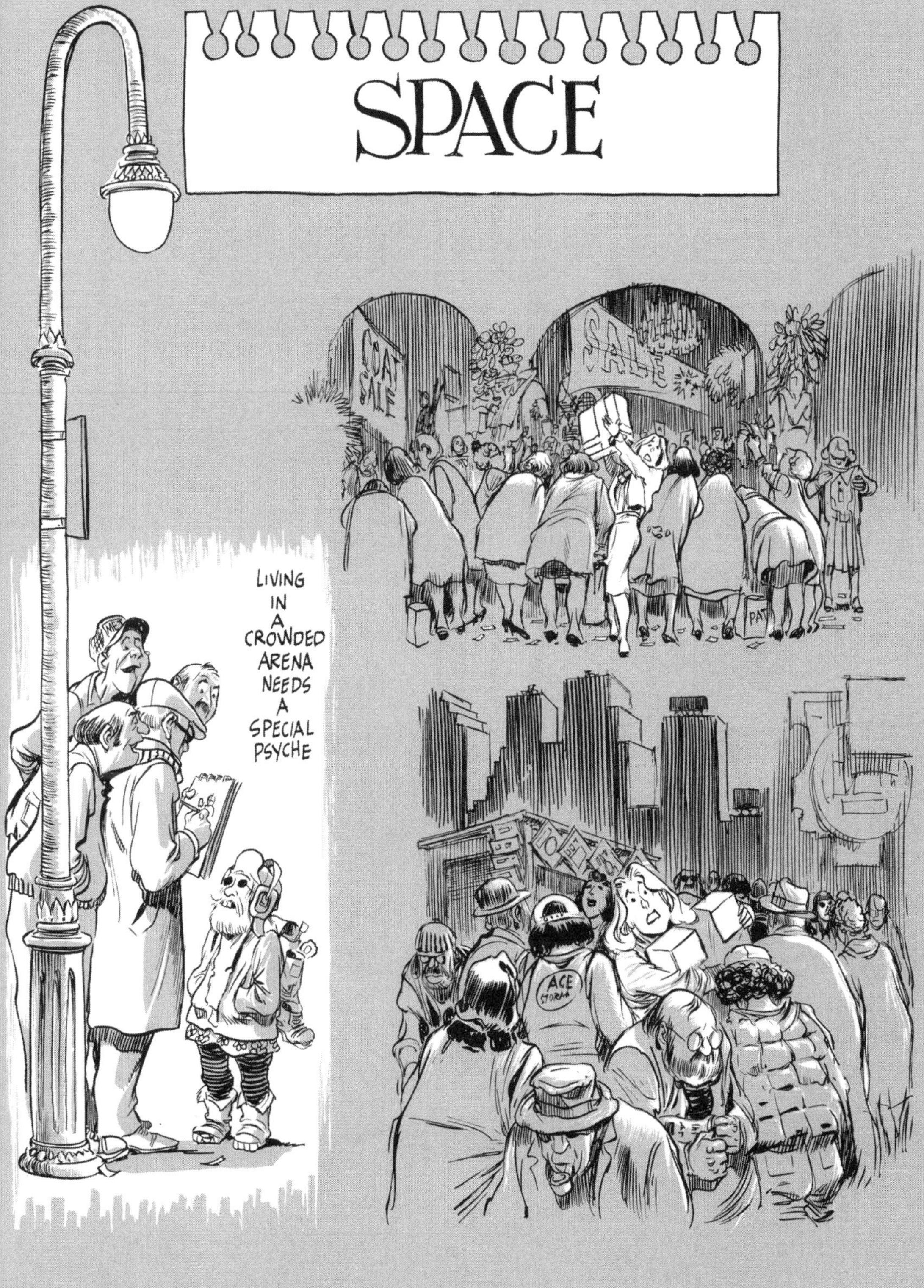
SPACE
LIVING IN A CROWDED ARENA NEEDS A SPECIAL PSYCHE
COAT SALE
SALE
ACE

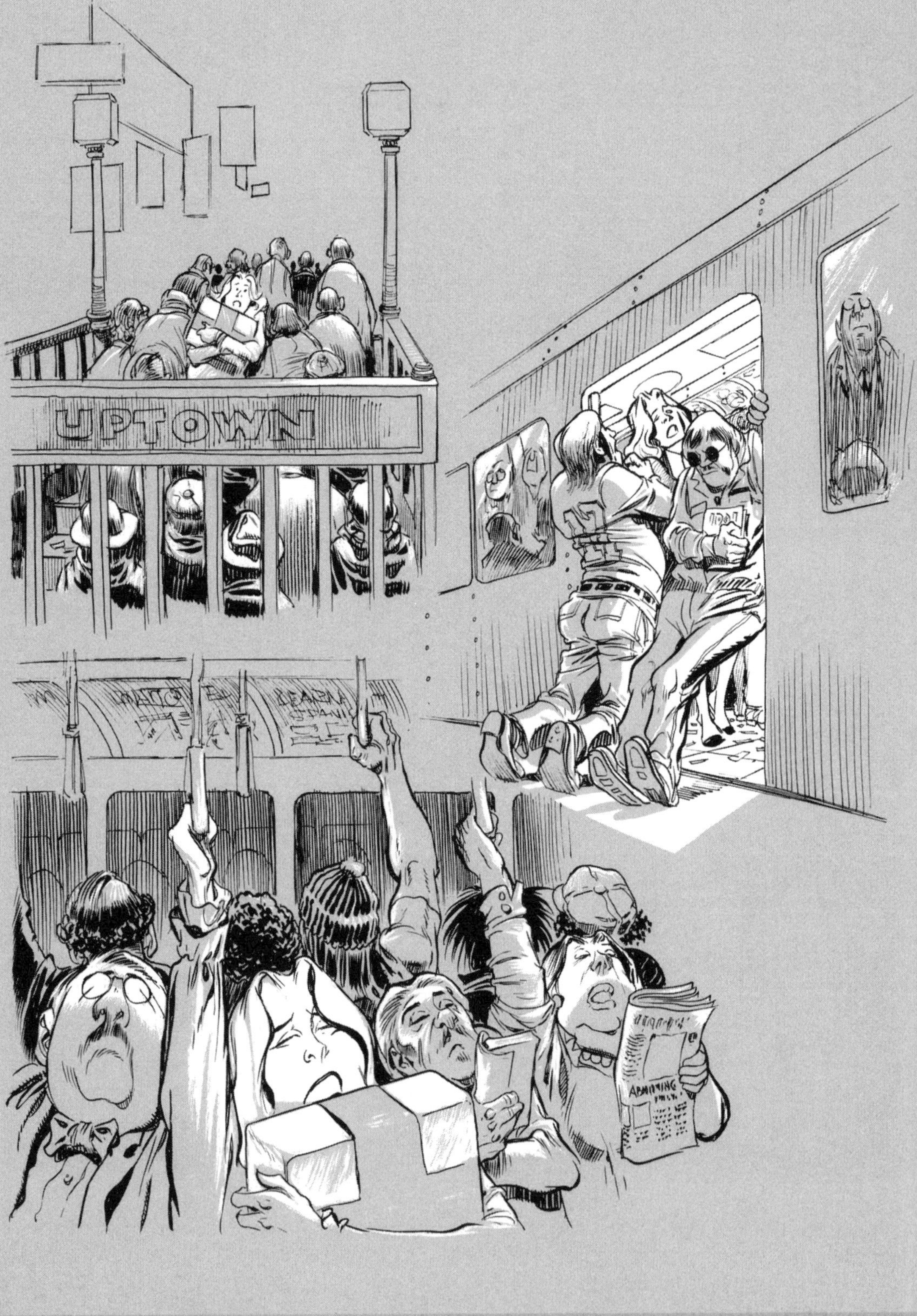
UPTOWN

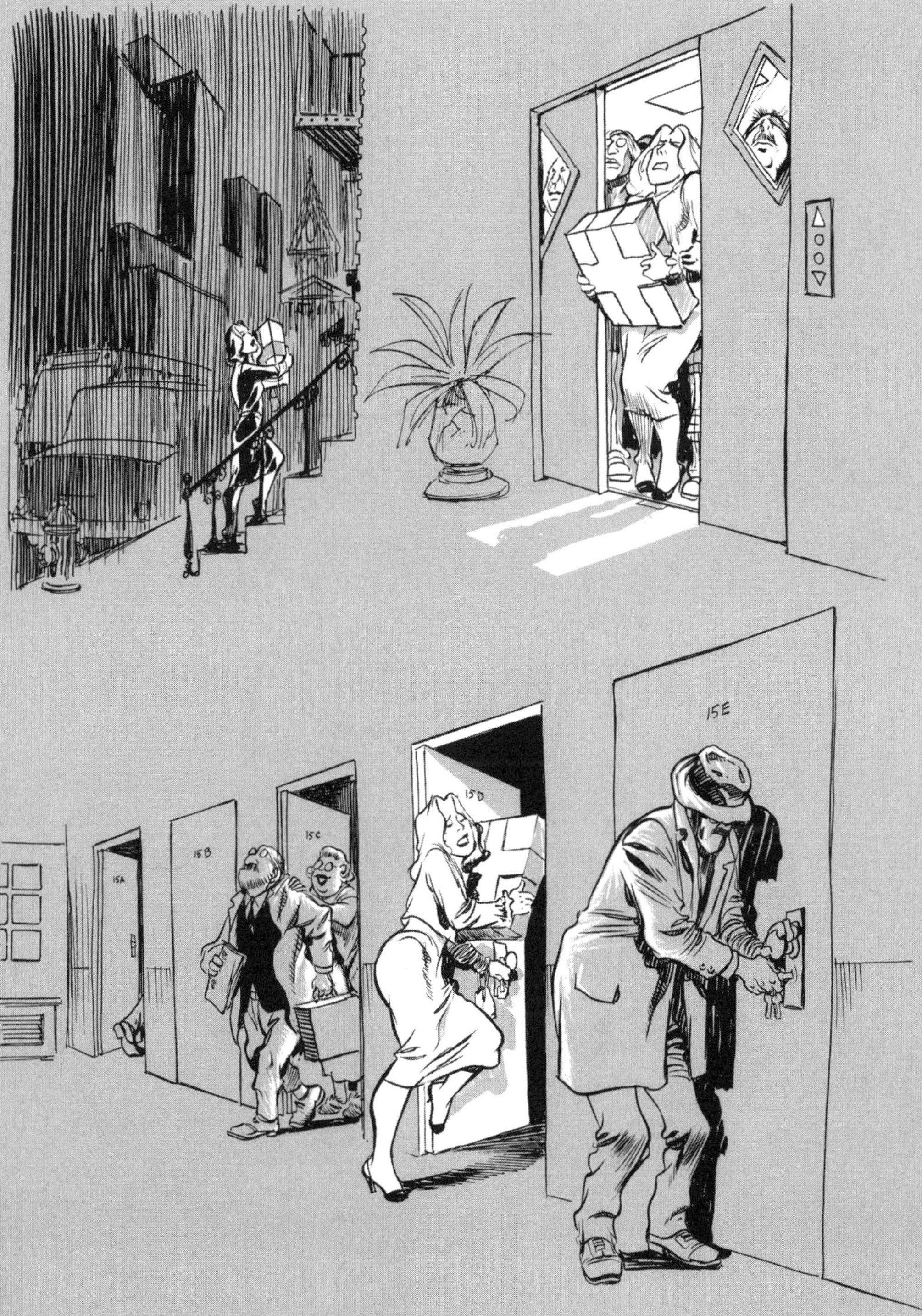
15A
15B
15C
15D
15E

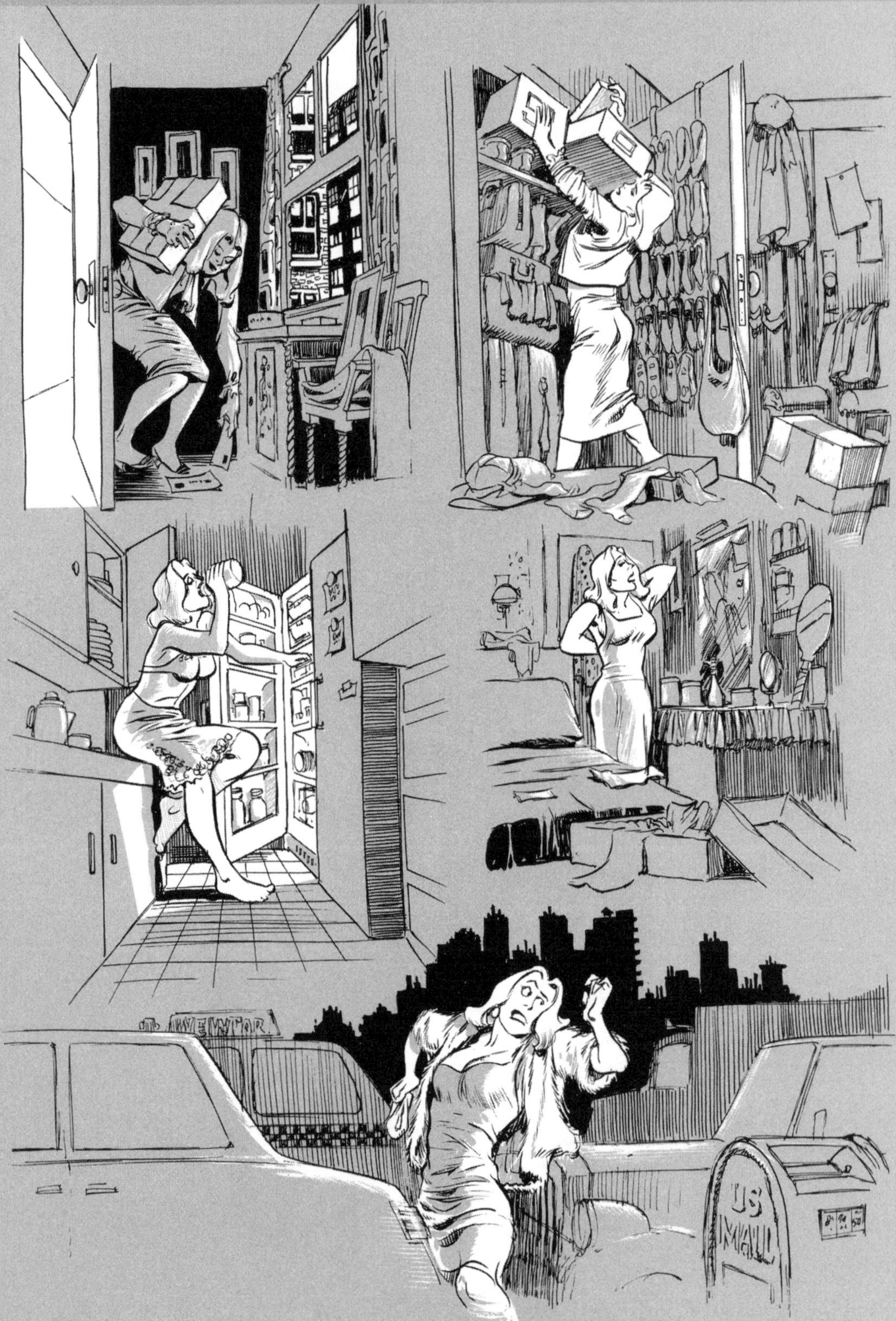
US
MAIL

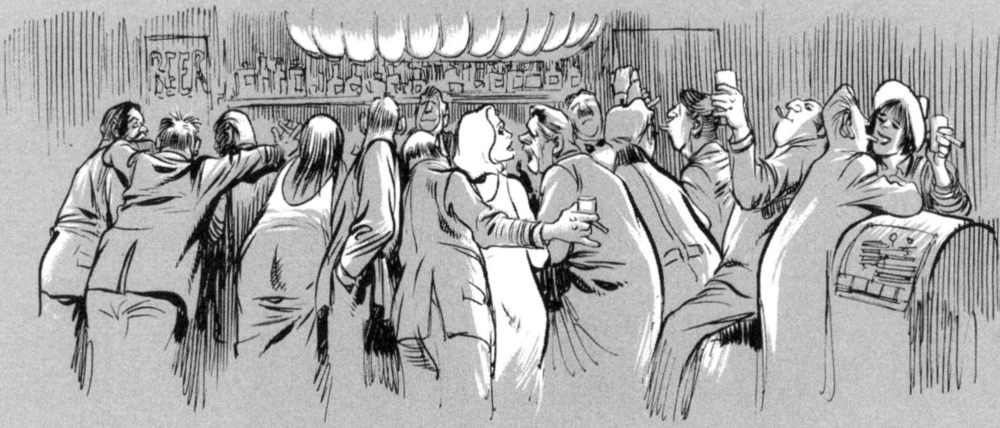
BEER

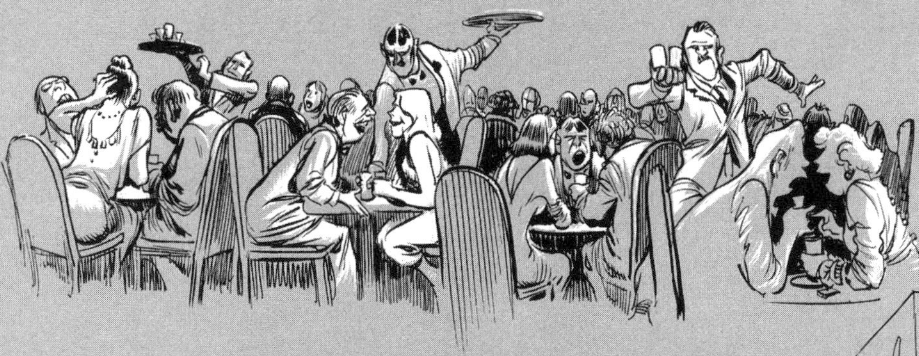

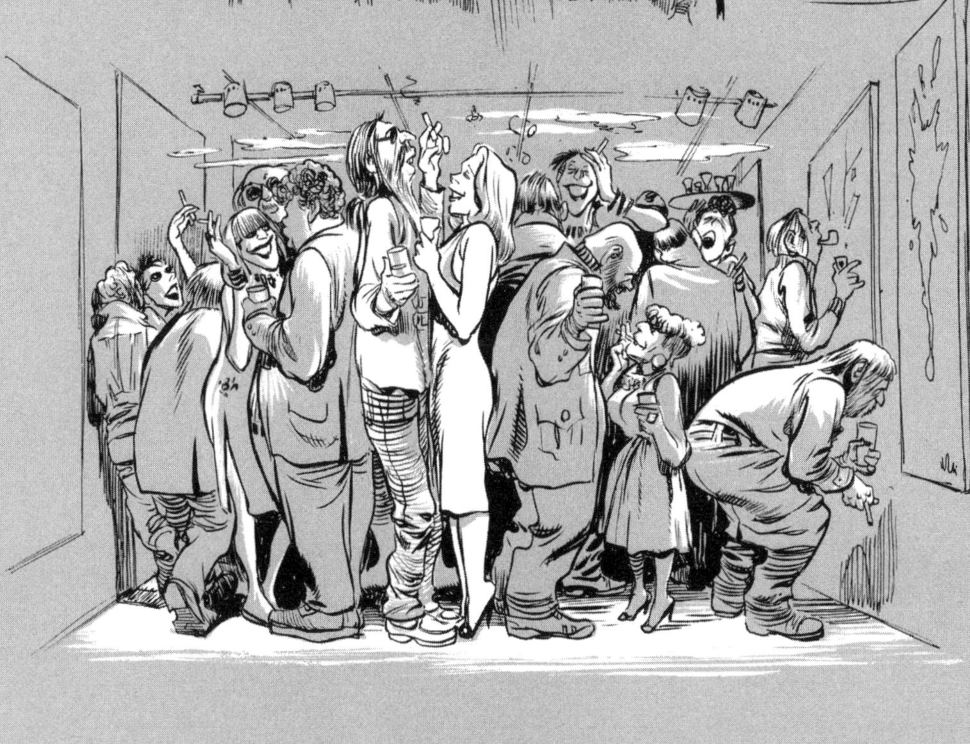

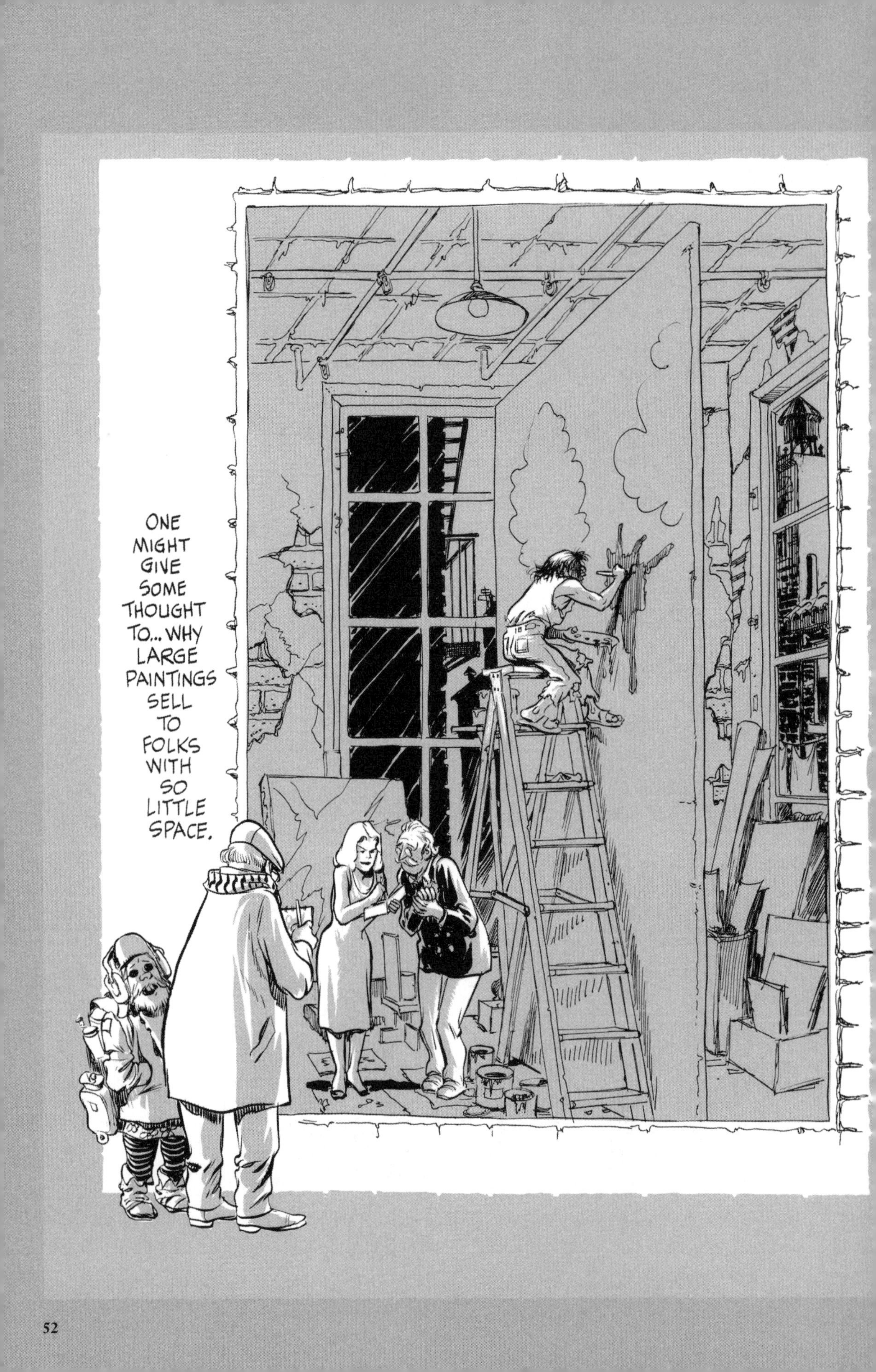
ONE MIGHT GIVE SOME THOUGHT TO... WHY LARGE PAINTINGS SELL TO FOLKS WITH SO LITTLE SPACE.

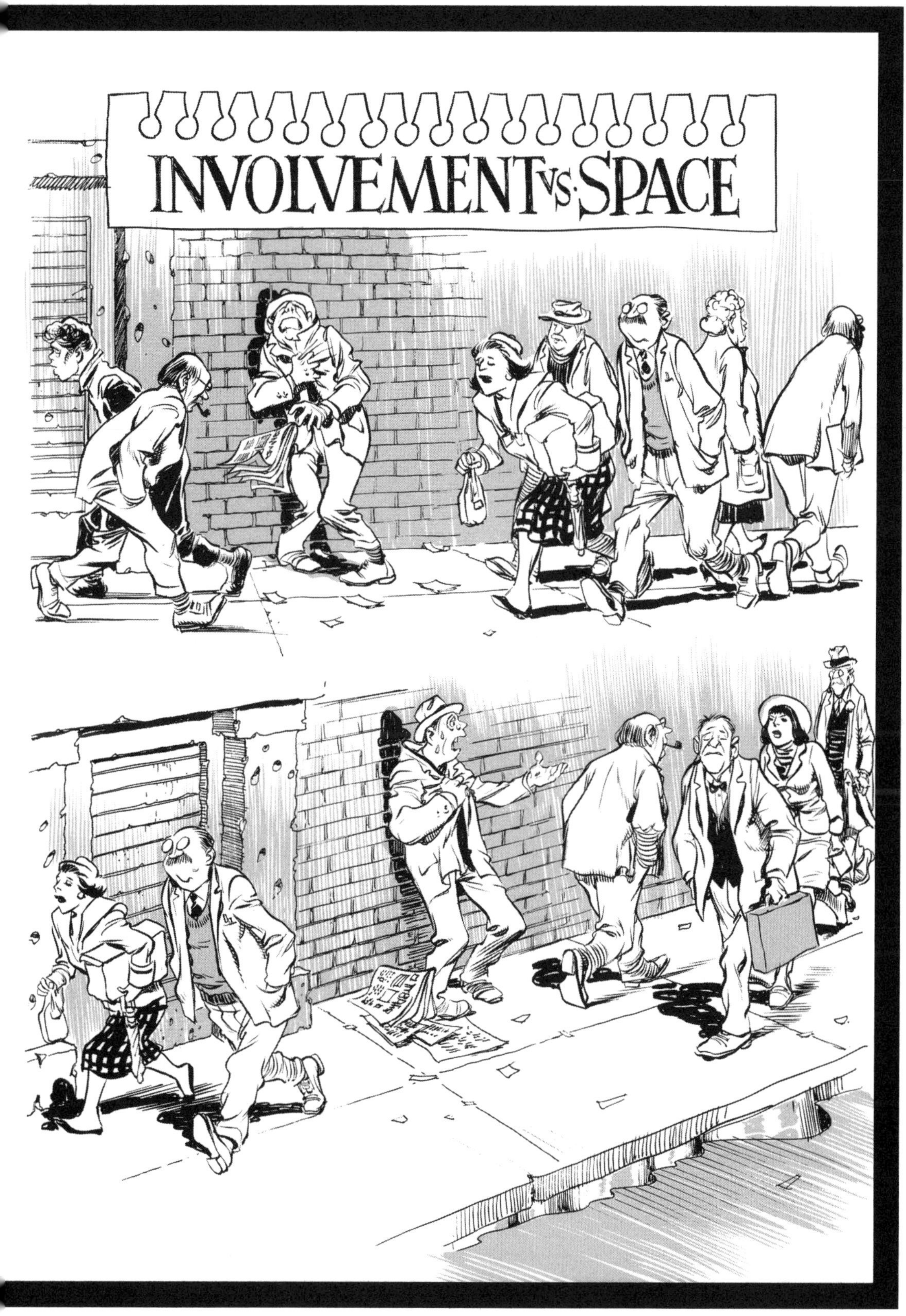
INVOLVEMENT VS. SPACE

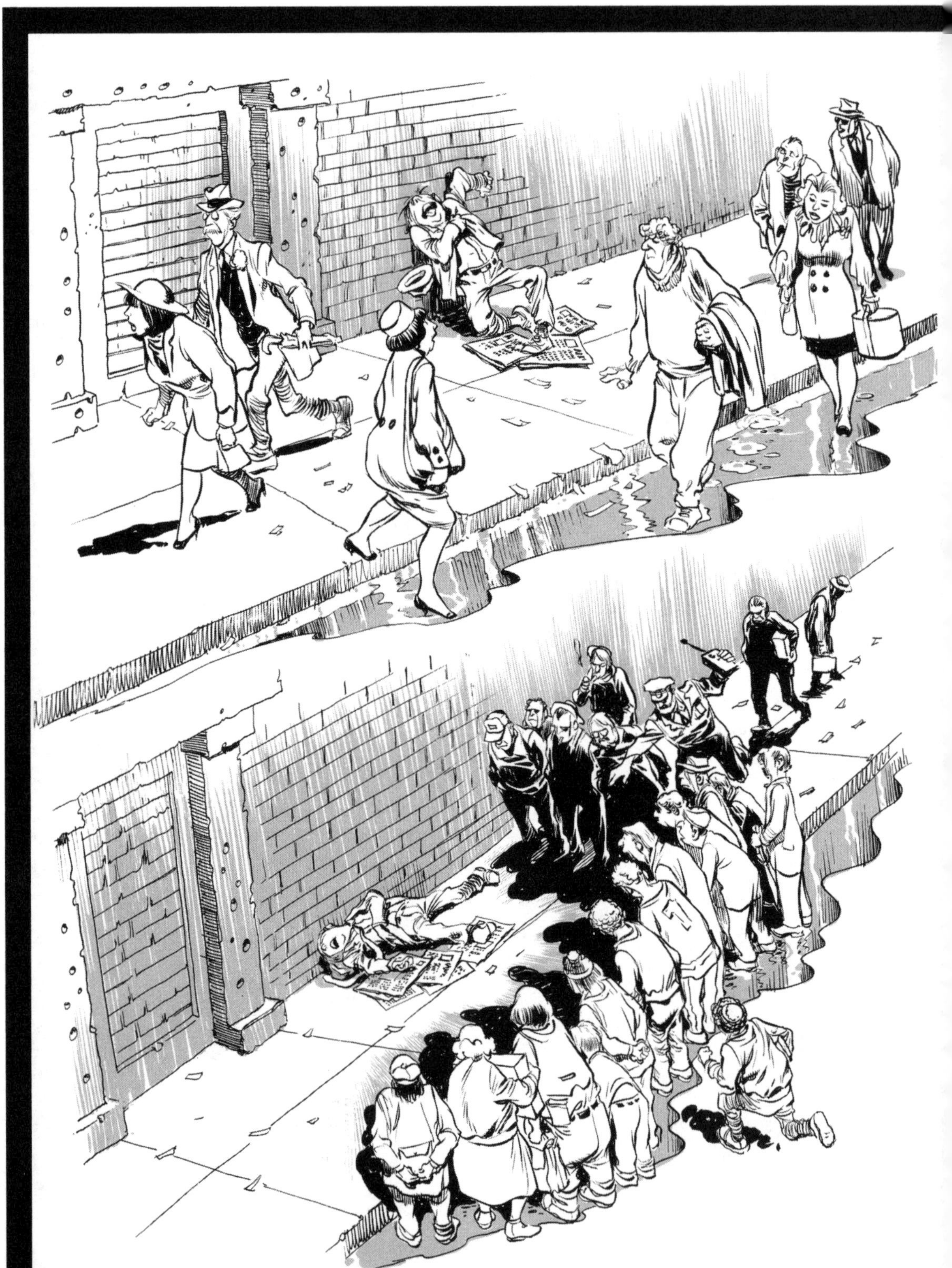

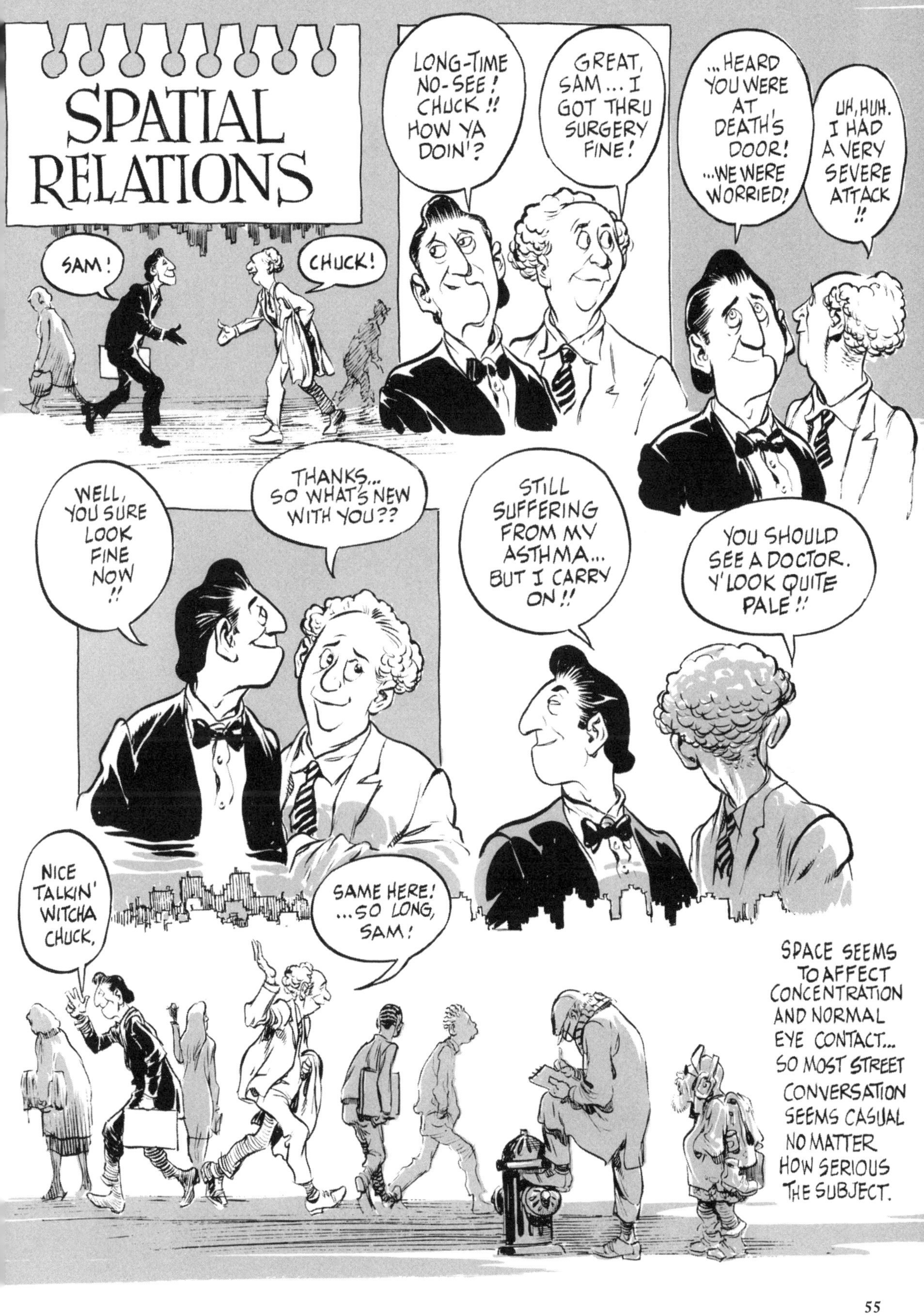
SPATIAL RELATIONS
SAM!
CHUCK!
LONG-TIME NO-SEE! CHUCK!! HOW YA DOIN'?
GREAT, SAM... I GOT THRU SURGERY FINE!
...HEARD YOU WERE AT DEATH'S DOOR! ...WE WERE WORRIED!
UH, HUH. I HAD A VERY SEVERE ATTACK!!
WELL, YOU SURE LOOK FINE NOW!!
THANKS... SO WHAT'S NEW WITH YOU??
STILL SUFFERING FROM MY ASTHMA... BUT I CARRY ON!!
YOU SHOULD SEE A DOCTOR. Y'LOOK QUITE PALE!!
NICE TALKIN' WITCHA CHUCK,
SAME HERE! ...SO LONG, SAM!
SPACE SEEMS TO AFFECT CONCENTRATION AND NORMAL EYE CONTACT... SO MOST STREET CONVERSATION SEEMS CASUAL NO MATTER HOW SERIOUS THE SUBJECT.

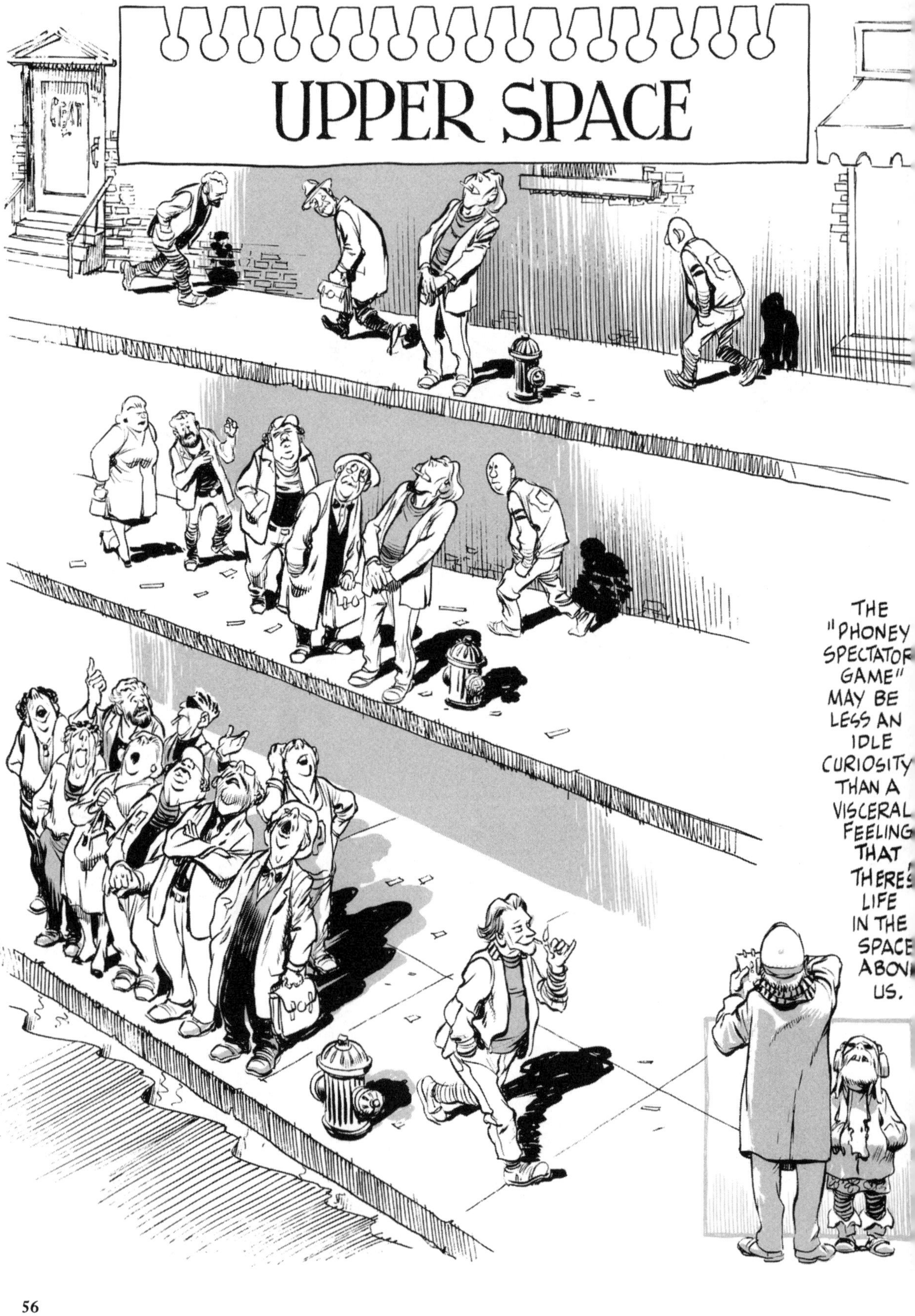
UPPER SPACE
THE "PHONEY SPECTATOR GAME" MAY BE LESS AN IDLE CURIOSITY THAN A VISCERAL FEELING THAT THERE'S LIFE IN THE SPACE ABOV US.

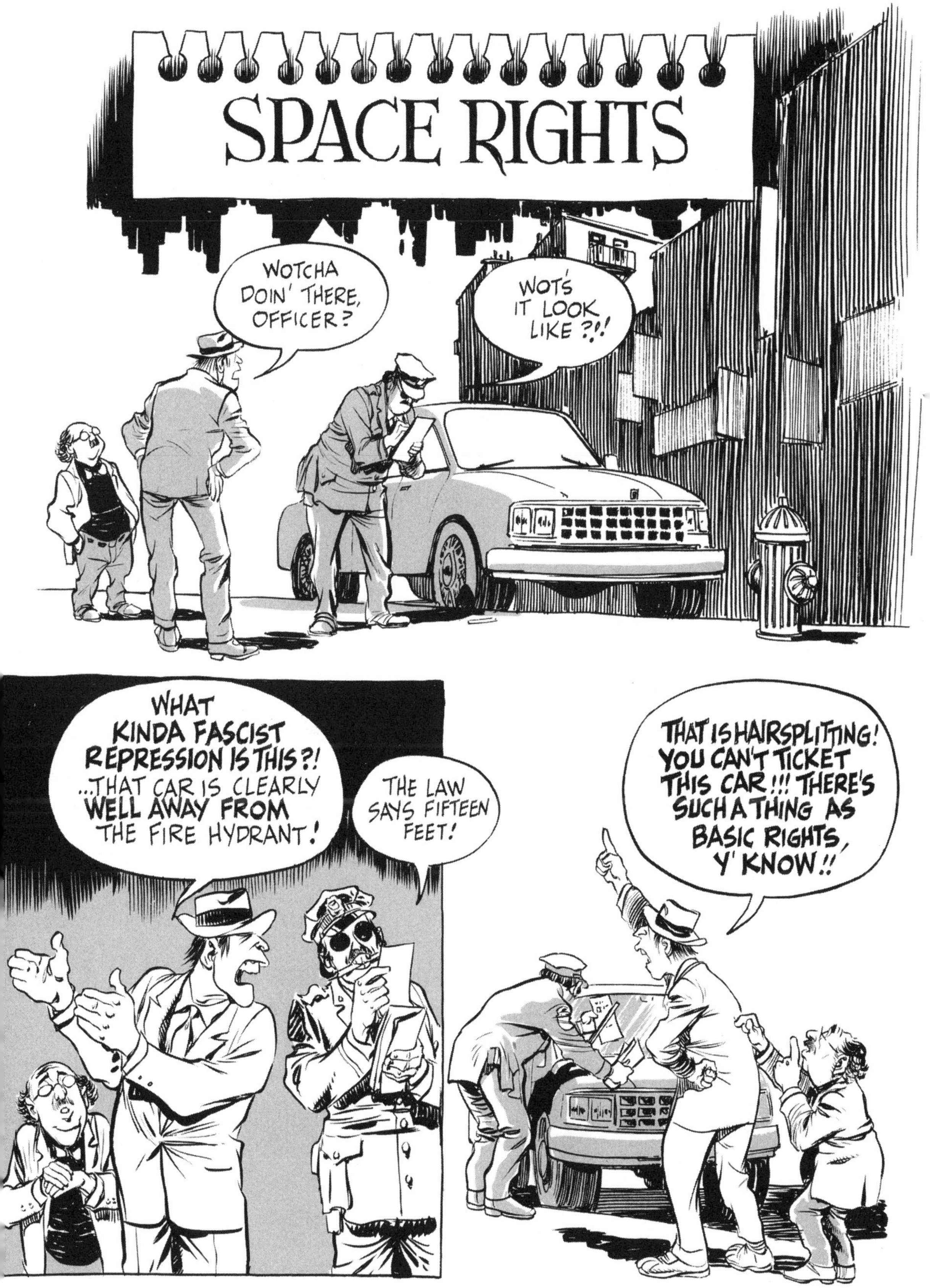
SPACE RIGHTS
WOTCHA DOIN' THERE, OFFICER?
WOT'S IT LOOK LIKE ?!!
WHAT KINDA FASCIST REPRESSION IS THIS?! ...THAT CAR IS CLEARLY WELL AWAY FROM THE FIRE HYDRANT!
THE LAW SAYS FIFTEEN FEET!
THAT IS HAIRSPLITTING! YOU CAN'T TICKET THIS CAR!!! THERE'S SUCH A THING AS BASIC RIGHTS, Y' KNOW!!

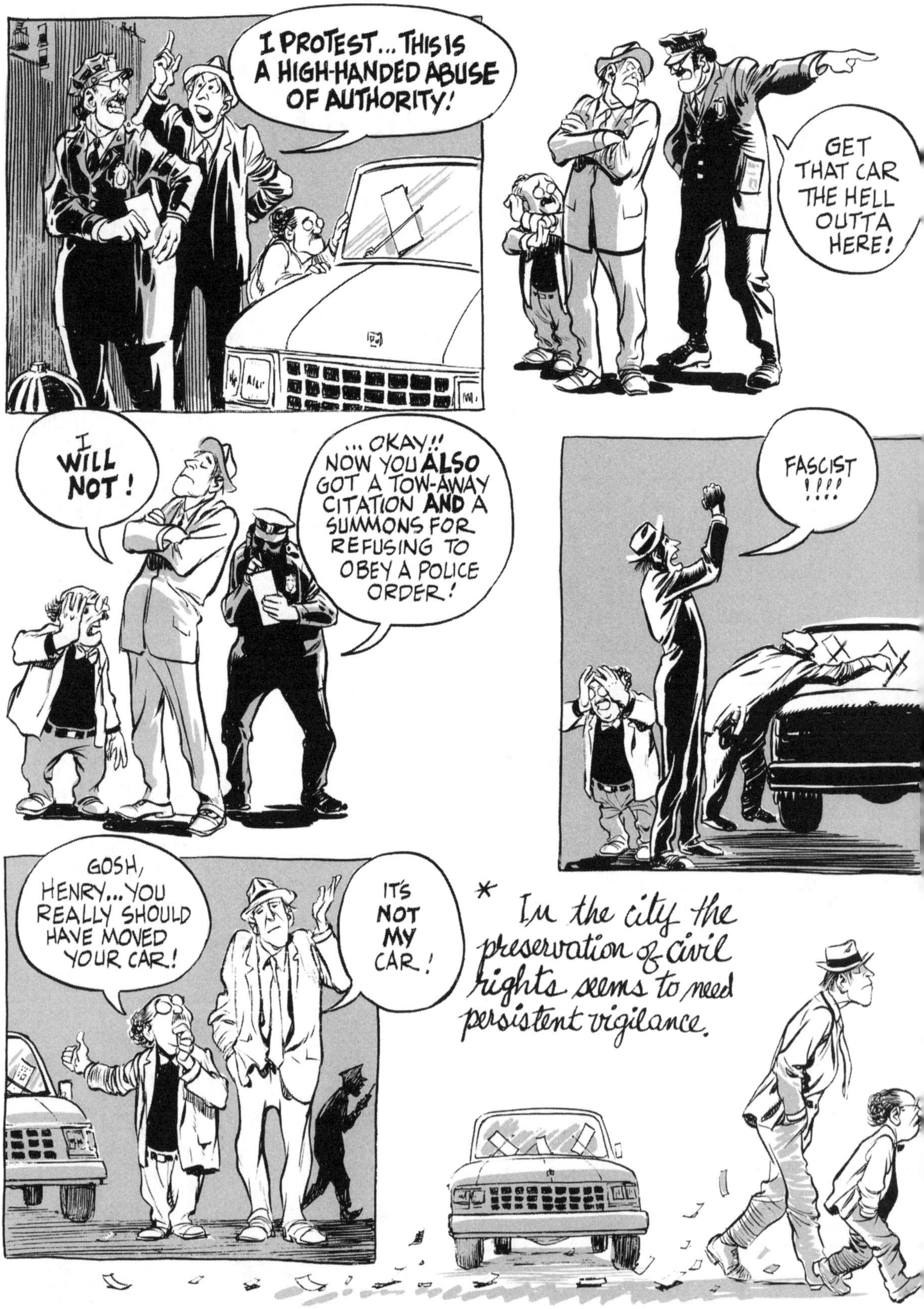
I PROTEST... THIS IS A HIGH-HANDED ABUSE OF AUTHORITY!
GET THAT CAR THE HELL OUTTA HERE!
I WILL NOT!
...OKAY!! NOW YOU ALSO GOT A TOW-AWAY CITATION AND A SUMMONS FOR REFUSING TO OBEY A POLICE ORDER!
FASCIST !!!!
GOSH, HENRY... YOU REALLY SHOULD HAVE MOVED YOUR CAR!
IT'S NOT MY CAR!
* In the city the preservation of civil rights seems to need persistent vigilance.

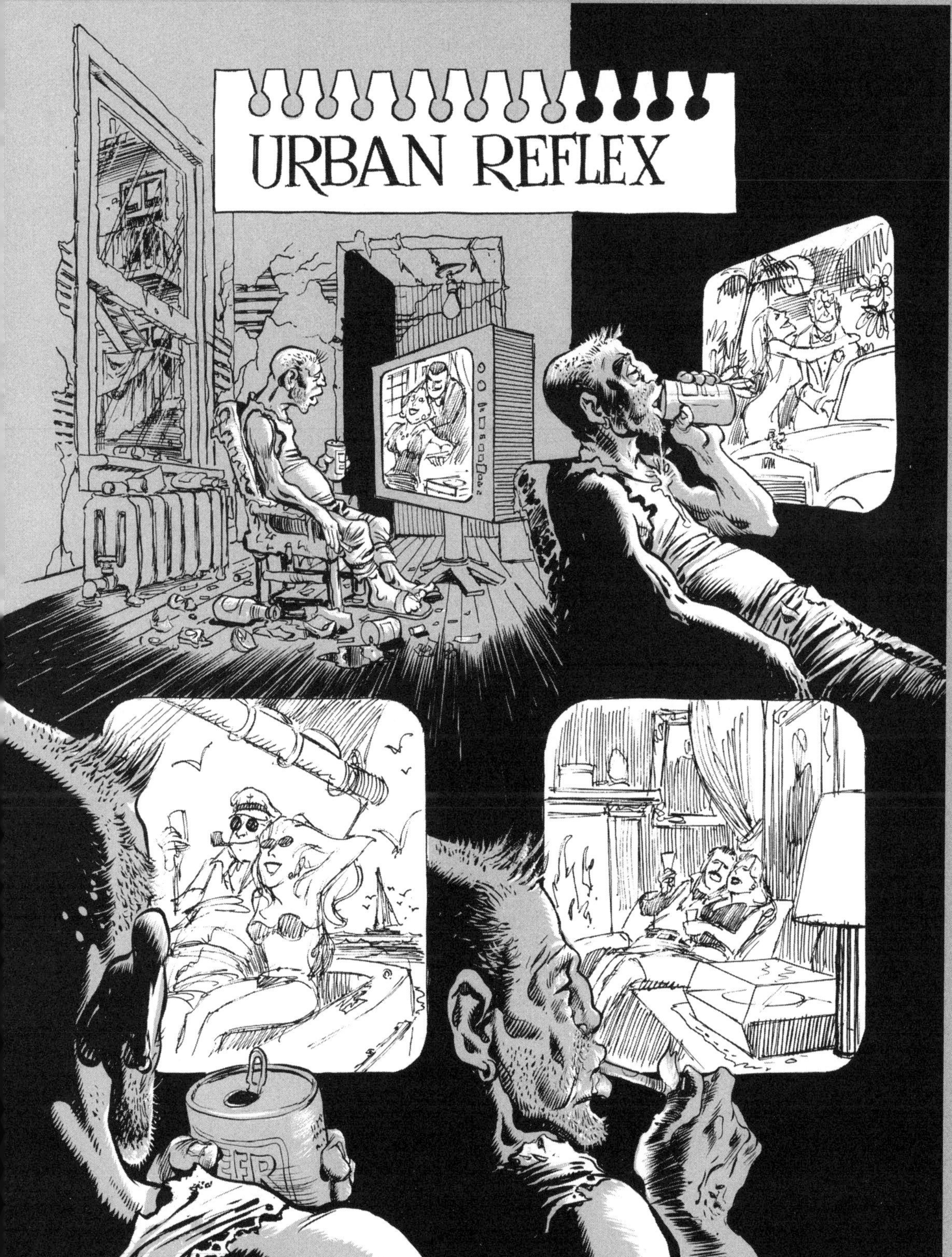
URBAN REFLEX

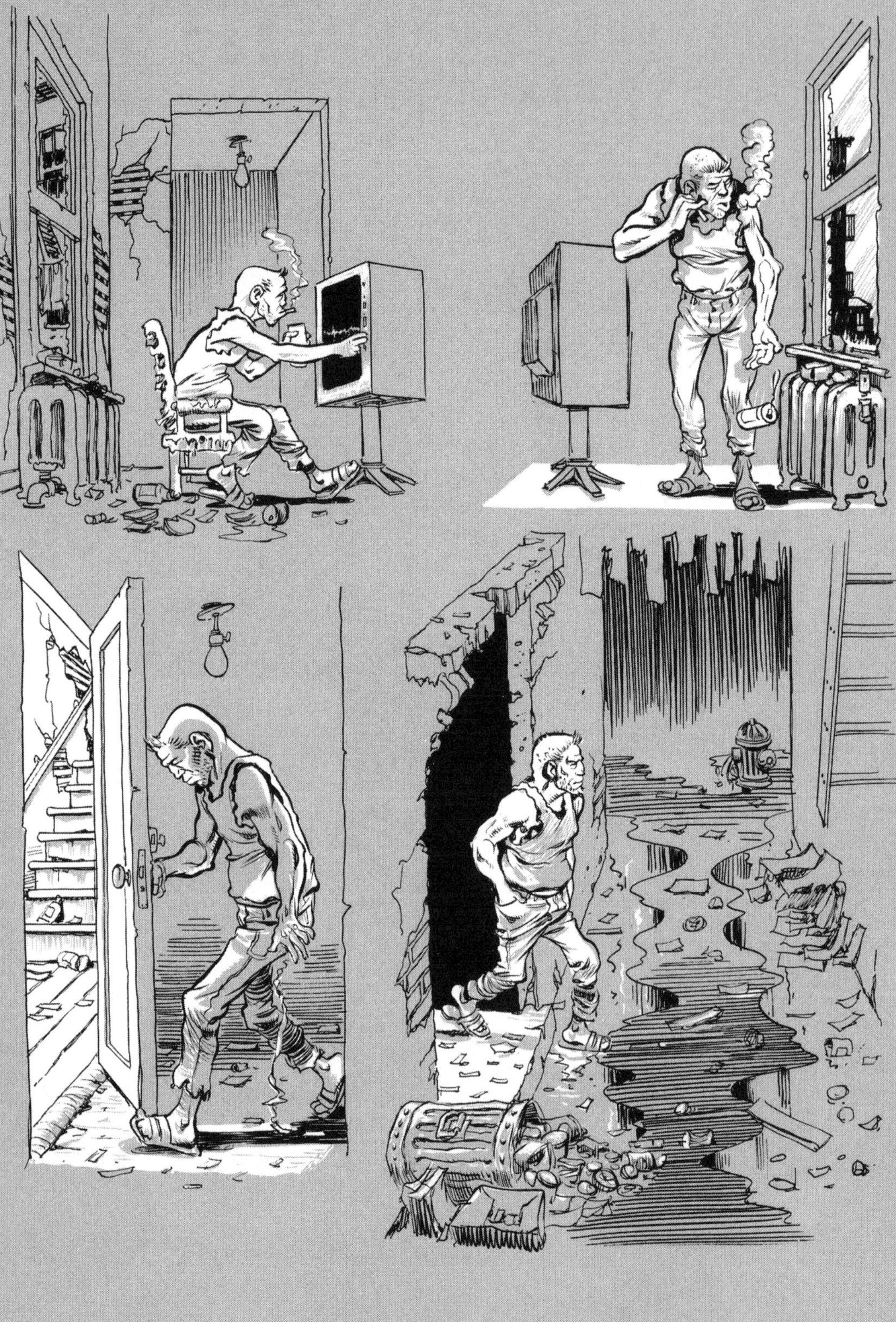

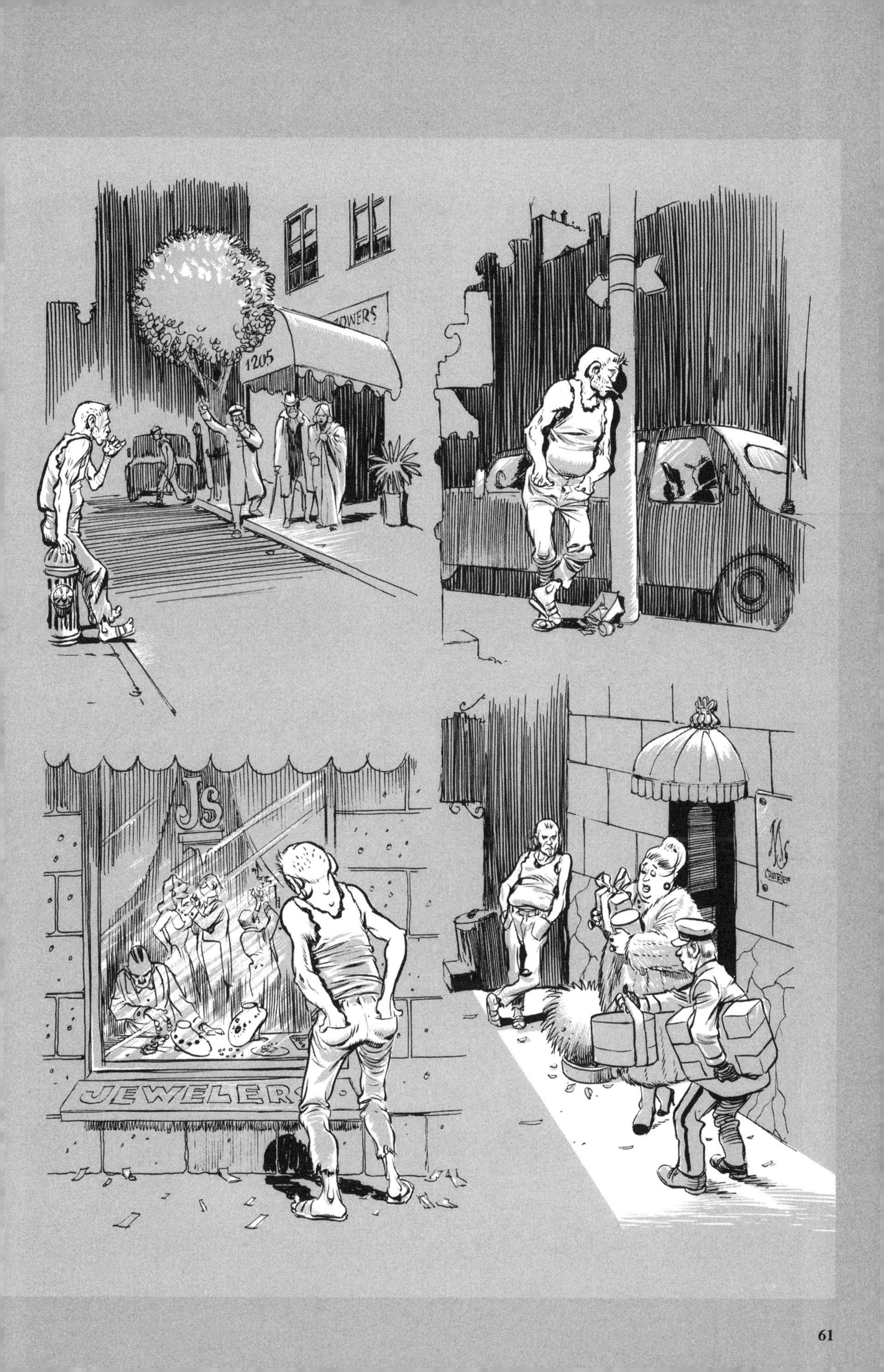
1205
JS

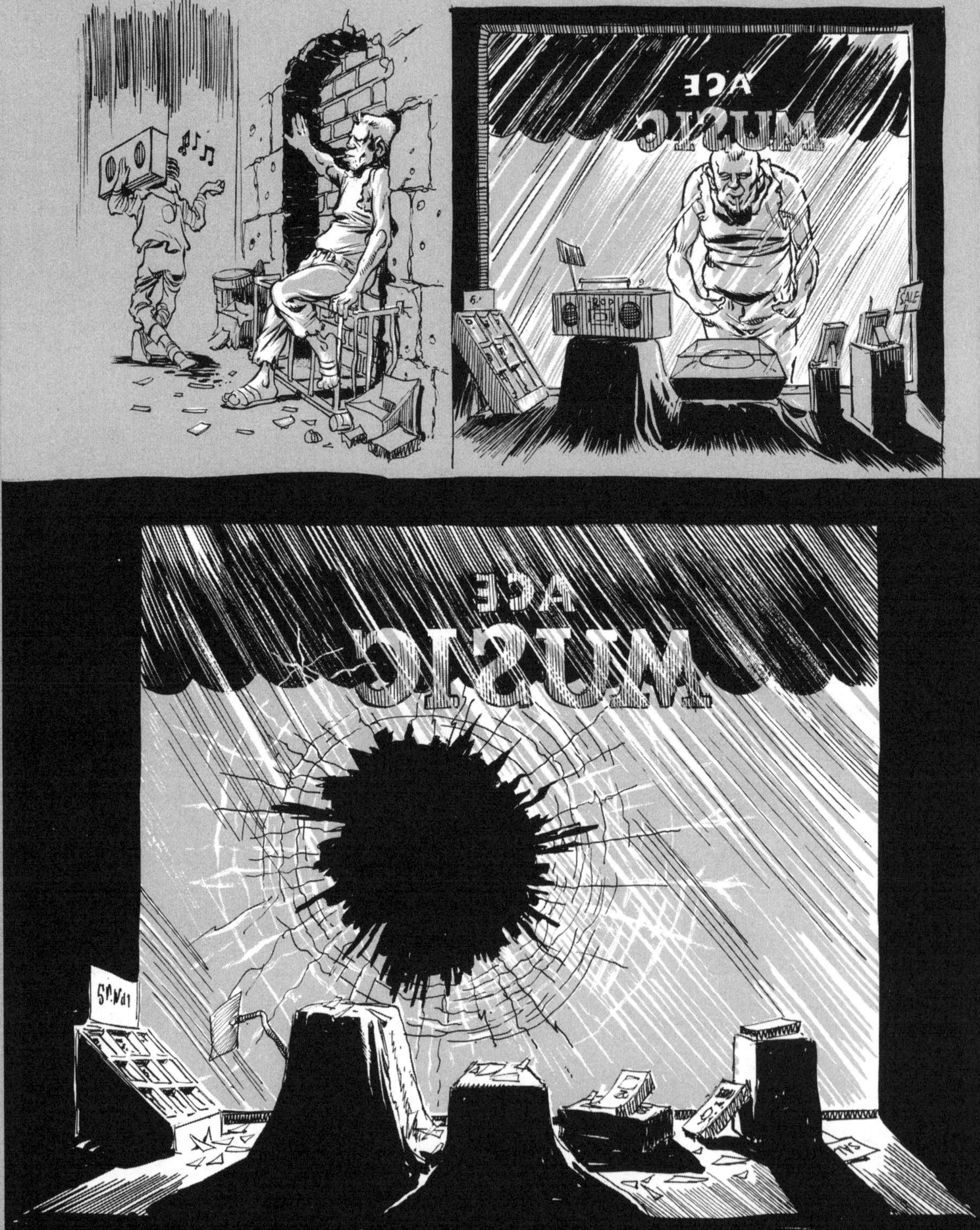
ACE
MUSIC
SALE
ACE
MUSIC

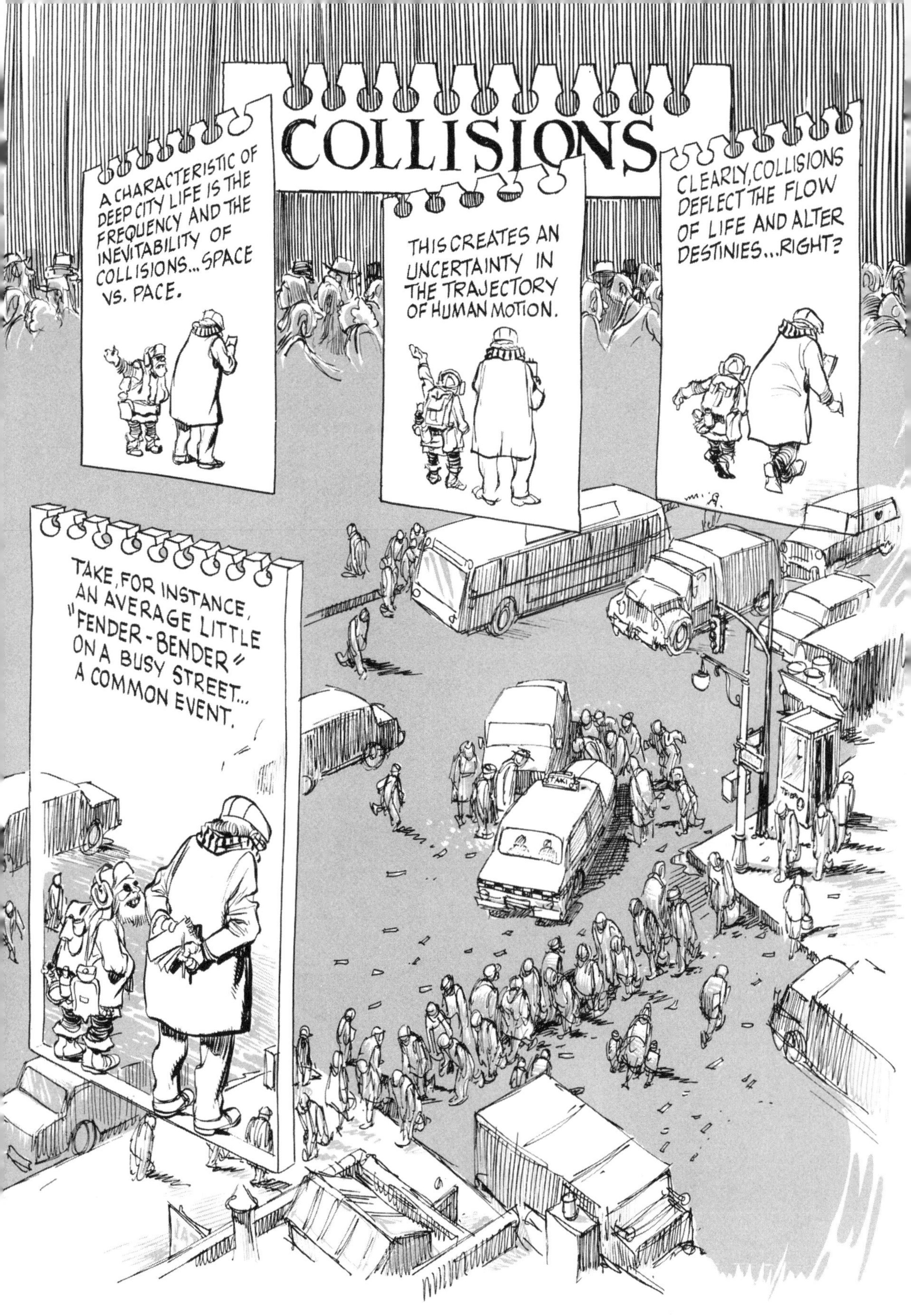
COLLISIONS
A CHARACTERISTIC OF DEEP CITY LIFE IS THE FREQUENCY AND THE INEVITABILITY OF COLLISIONS... SPACE VS. PACE.
THIS CREATES AN UNCERTAINTY IN THE TRAJECTORY OF HUMAN MOTION.
CLEARLY, COLLISIONS DEFLECT THE FLOW OF LIFE AND ALTER DESTINIES... RIGHT?
TAKE, FOR INSTANCE, AN AVERAGE LITTLE "FENDER-BENDER" ON A BUSY STREET... A COMMON EVENT.
TAXI

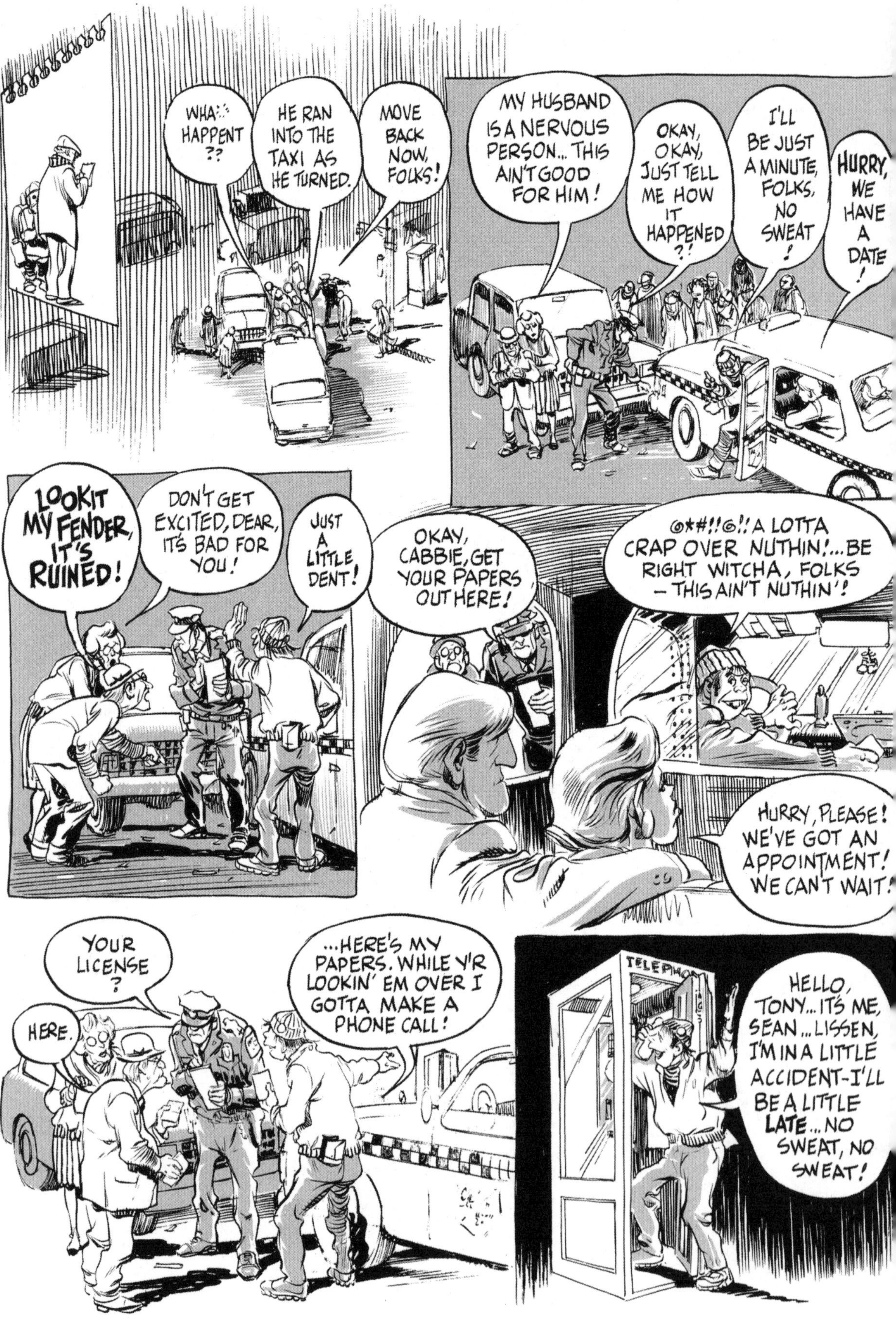

WHA... HAPPENT ??
HE RAN INTO THE TAXI AS HE TURNED.
MOVE BACK NOW, FOLKS!
MY HUSBAND IS A NERVOUS PERSON... THIS AIN'T GOOD FOR HIM!
OKAY, OKAY, JUST TELL ME HOW IT HAPPENED ?!
I'LL BE JUST A MINUTE, FOLKS, NO SWEAT!
HURRY, WE HAVE A DATE!
LOOKIT MY FENDER, IT'S RUINED!
DON'T GET EXCITED, DEAR, IT'S BAD FOR YOU!
JUST A LITTLE DENT!
OKAY, CABBIE, GET YOUR PAPERS OUT HERE!
@*#!!@!! A LOTTA CRAP OVER NUTHIN'!...BE RIGHT WITCHA, FOLKS — THIS AIN'T NUTHIN'!
HURRY, PLEASE! WE'VE GOT AN APPOINTMENT! WE CAN'T WAIT!
YOUR LICENSE ?
HERE.
...HERE'S MY PAPERS. WHILE Y'R LOOKIN' EM OVER I GOTTA MAKE A PHONE CALL!
HELLO, TONY... IT'S ME, SEAN... LISSEN, I'M IN A LITTLE ACCIDENT-I'LL BE A LITTLE LATE... NO SWEAT, NO SWEAT!

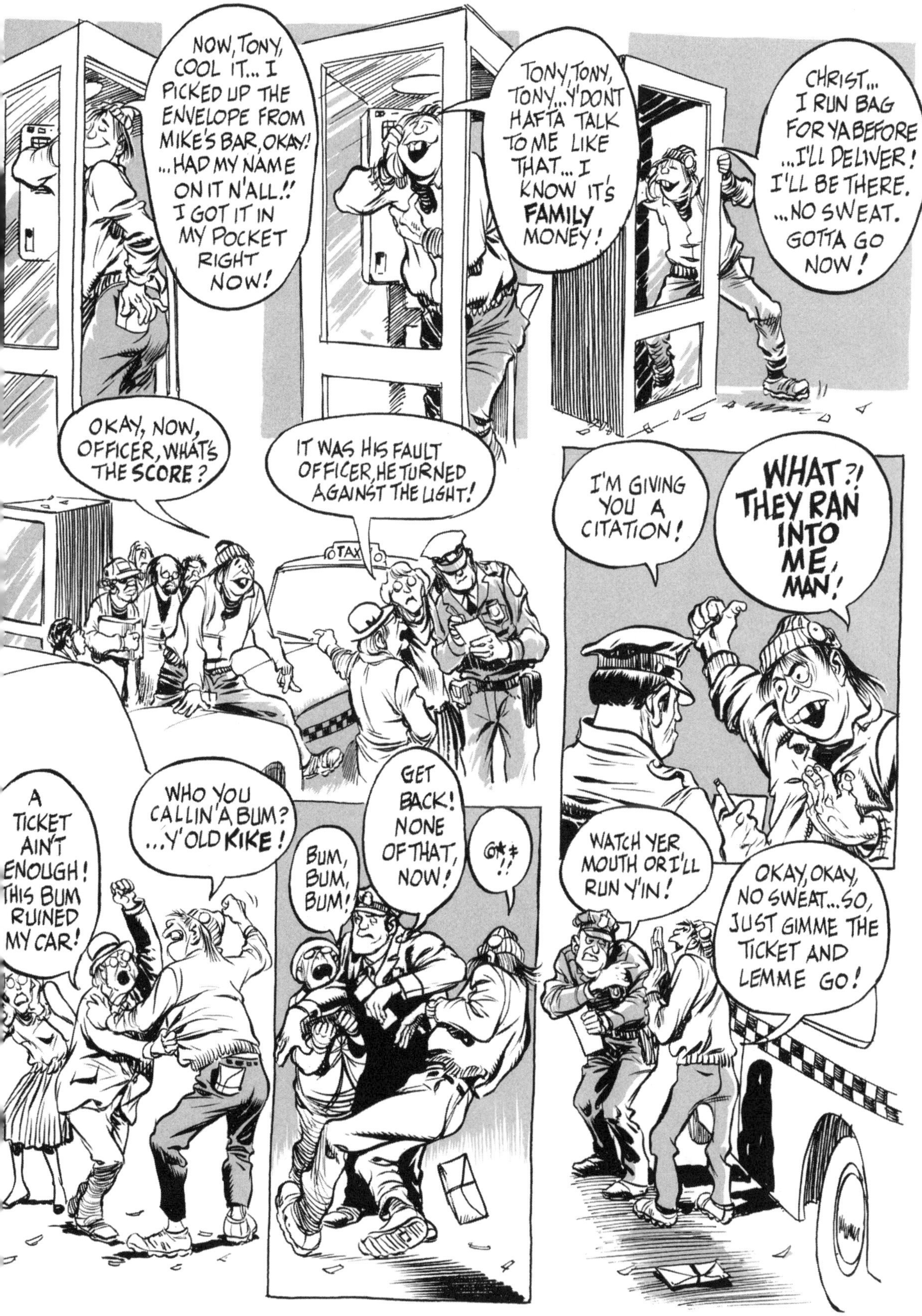
NOW, TONY, COOL IT... I PICKED UP THE ENVELOPE FROM MIKE'S BAR, OKAY! ...HAD MY NAME ON IT N'ALL!! I GOT IT IN MY POCKET RIGHT NOW!
TONY, TONY, TONY... Y'DONT HAFTA TALK TO ME LIKE THAT... I KNOW IT'S FAMILY MONEY!
CHRIST... I RUN BAG FOR YA BEFORE ...I'LL DELIVER! I'LL BE THERE. ...NO SWEAT. GOTTA GO NOW!
OKAY, NOW, OFFICER, WHAT'S THE SCORE?
IT WAS HIS FAULT OFFICER, HE TURNED AGAINST THE LIGHT!
TAXI
I'M GIVING YOU A CITATION!
WHAT?! THEY RAN INTO ME, MAN!
A TICKET AIN'T ENOUGH! THIS BUM RUINED MY CAR!
WHO YOU CALLIN' A BUM? ...Y'OLD KIKE!
BUM, BUM, BUM!
GET BACK! NONE OF THAT, NOW!
@*‡ !!
WATCH YER MOUTH OR I'LL RUN Y'IN!
OKAY, OKAY, NO SWEAT... SO, JUST GIMME THE TICKET AND LEMME GO!

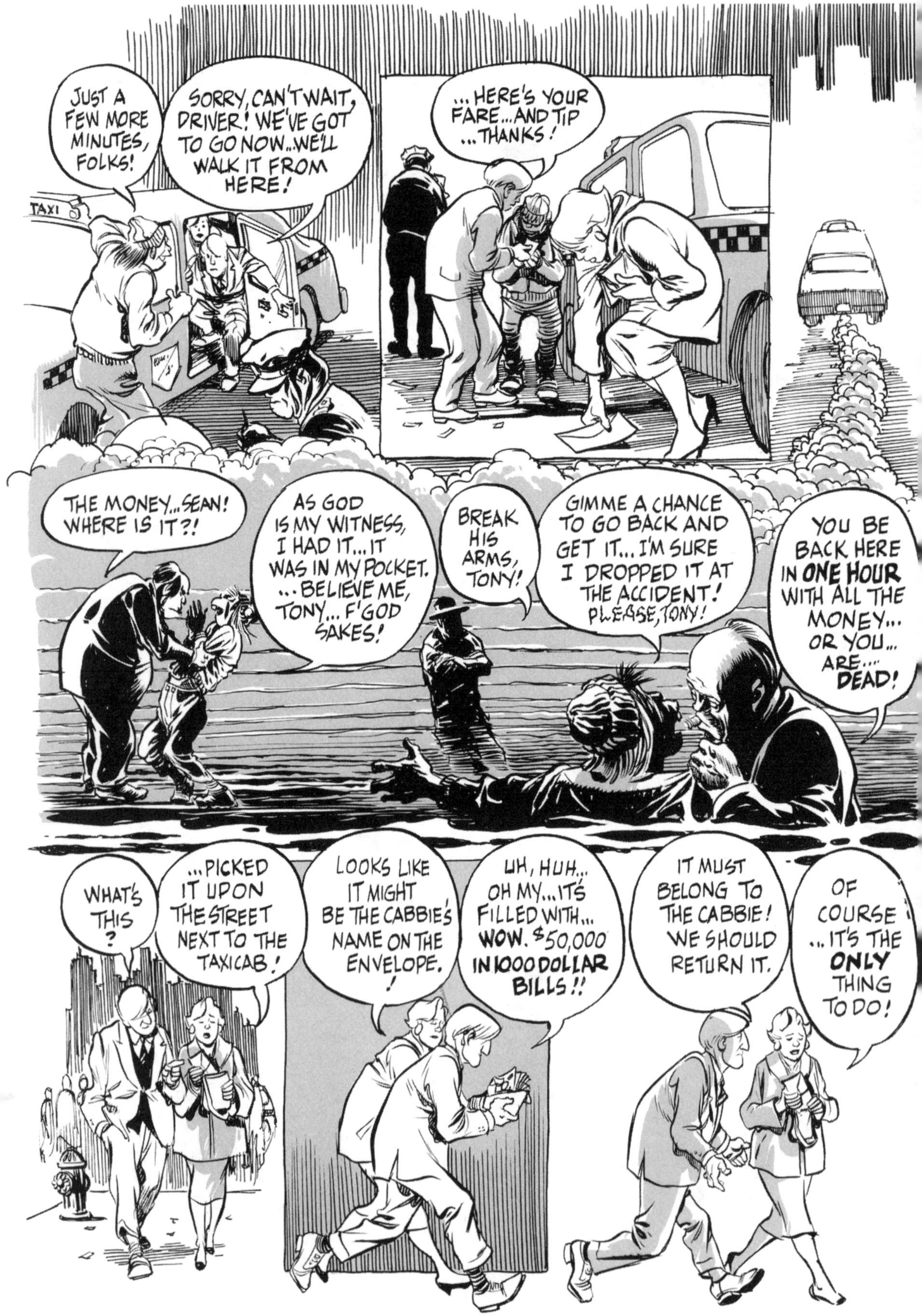

JUST A FEW MORE MINUTES, FOLKS!
SORRY, CAN'T WAIT, DRIVER! WE'VE GOT TO GO NOW..WE'LL WALK IT FROM HERE!
TAXI
... HERE'S YOUR FARE...AND TIP ... THANKS!
THE MONEY...SEAN! WHERE IS IT?!
AS GOD IS MY WITNESS, I HAD IT... IT WAS IN MY POCKET. ... BELIEVE ME, TONY... F'GOD SAKES!
BREAK HIS ARMS, TONY!
GIMME A CHANCE TO GO BACK AND GET IT... I'M SURE I DROPPED IT AT THE ACCIDENT! PLEASE, TONY!
YOU BE BACK HERE IN ONE HOUR WITH ALL THE MONEY... OR YOU... ARE.... DEAD!
WHAT'S THIS ?
...PICKED IT UP ON THE STREET NEXT TO THE TAXICAB!
LOOKS LIKE IT MIGHT BE THE CABBIE'S NAME ON THE ENVELOPE. !
UH, HUH... OH MY... IT'S FILLED WITH... WOW. $50,000 IN 1000 DOLLAR BILLS!!
IT MUST BELONG TO THE CABBIE! WE SHOULD RETURN IT.
OF COURSE ... IT'S THE ONLY THING TO DO!

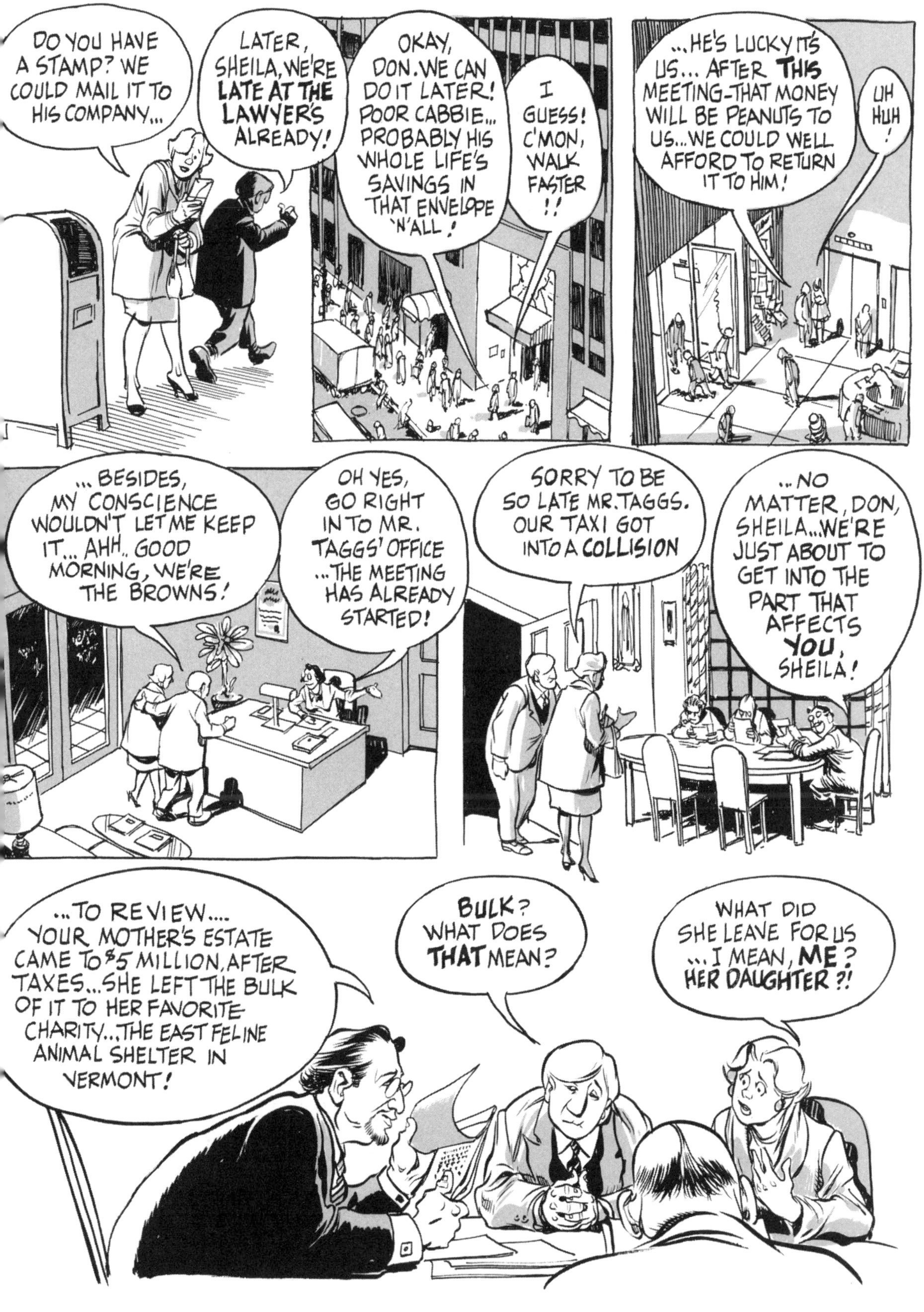
DO YOU HAVE A STAMP? WE COULD MAIL IT TO HIS COMPANY...
LATER, SHEILA, WE'RE LATE AT THE LAWYER'S ALREADY!
OKAY, DON. WE CAN DO IT LATER! POOR CABBIE... PROBABLY HIS WHOLE LIFE'S SAVINGS IN THAT ENVELOPE 'N'ALL!
I GUESS! C'MON, WALK FASTER!!
...HE'S LUCKY IT'S US... AFTER THIS MEETING-THAT MONEY WILL BE PEANUTS TO US...WE COULD WELL AFFORD TO RETURN IT TO HIM!
UH HUH!
...BESIDES, MY CONSCIENCE WOULDN'T LET ME KEEP IT... AHH.. GOOD MORNING, WE'RE THE BROWNS!
OH YES, GO RIGHT IN TO MR. TAGGS' OFFICE ...THE MEETING HAS ALREADY STARTED!
SORRY TO BE SO LATE MR. TAGGS. OUR TAXI GOT INTO A COLLISION
..NO MATTER, DON, SHEILA...WE'RE JUST ABOUT TO GET INTO THE PART THAT AFFECTS YOU, SHEILA!
...TO REVIEW.... YOUR MOTHER'S ESTATE CAME TO $5 MILLION, AFTER TAXES...SHE LEFT THE BULK OF IT TO HER FAVORITE CHARITY...THE EAST FELINE ANIMAL SHELTER IN VERMONT!
BULK? WHAT DOES THAT MEAN?
WHAT DID SHE LEAVE FOR US ...I MEAN, ME? HER DAUGHTER?!

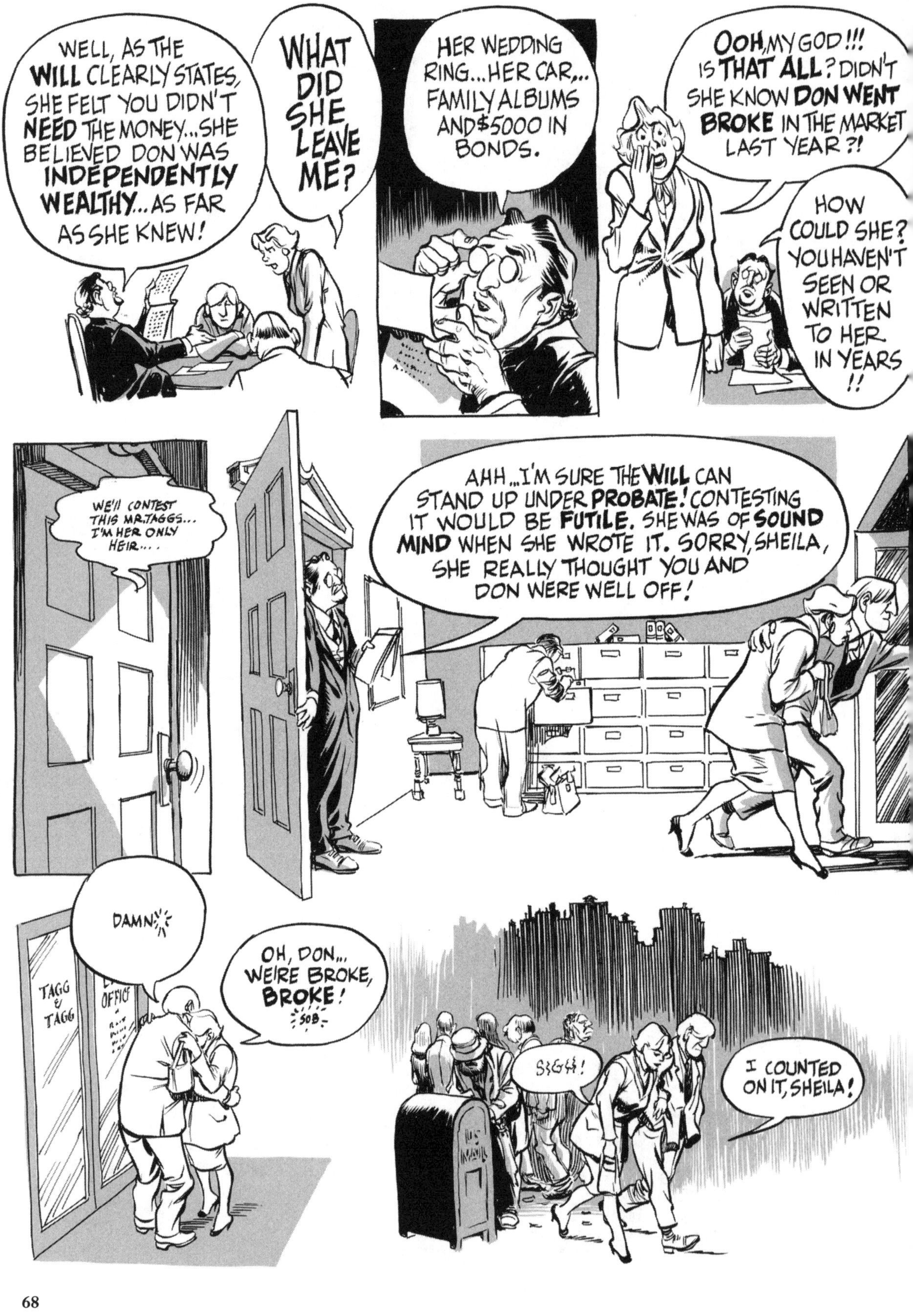
WELL, AS THE WILL CLEARLY STATES, SHE FELT YOU DIDN'T NEED THE MONEY...SHE BELIEVED DON WAS INDEPENDENTLY WEALTHY...AS FAR AS SHE KNEW!
WHAT DID SHE LEAVE ME?
HER WEDDING RING...HER CAR,... FAMILY ALBUMS AND $5000 IN BONDS.
OOH, MY GOD!!! IS THAT ALL? DIDN'T SHE KNOW DON WENT BROKE IN THE MARKET LAST YEAR?!
HOW COULD SHE? YOU HAVEN'T SEEN OR WRITTEN TO HER IN YEARS!!
WE'LL CONTEST THIS MR. TAGGS... I'M HER ONLY HEIR....
AHH...I'M SURE THE WILL CAN STAND UP UNDER PROBATE! CONTESTING IT WOULD BE FUTILE. SHE WAS OF SOUND MIND WHEN SHE WROTE IT. SORRY, SHEILA, SHE REALLY THOUGHT YOU AND DON WERE WELL OFF!
DAMN!
TAGG & TAGG
OFFICE
OH, DON... WE'RE BROKE, BROKE!
SOB
SIGH!
I COUNTED ON IT, SHEILA!

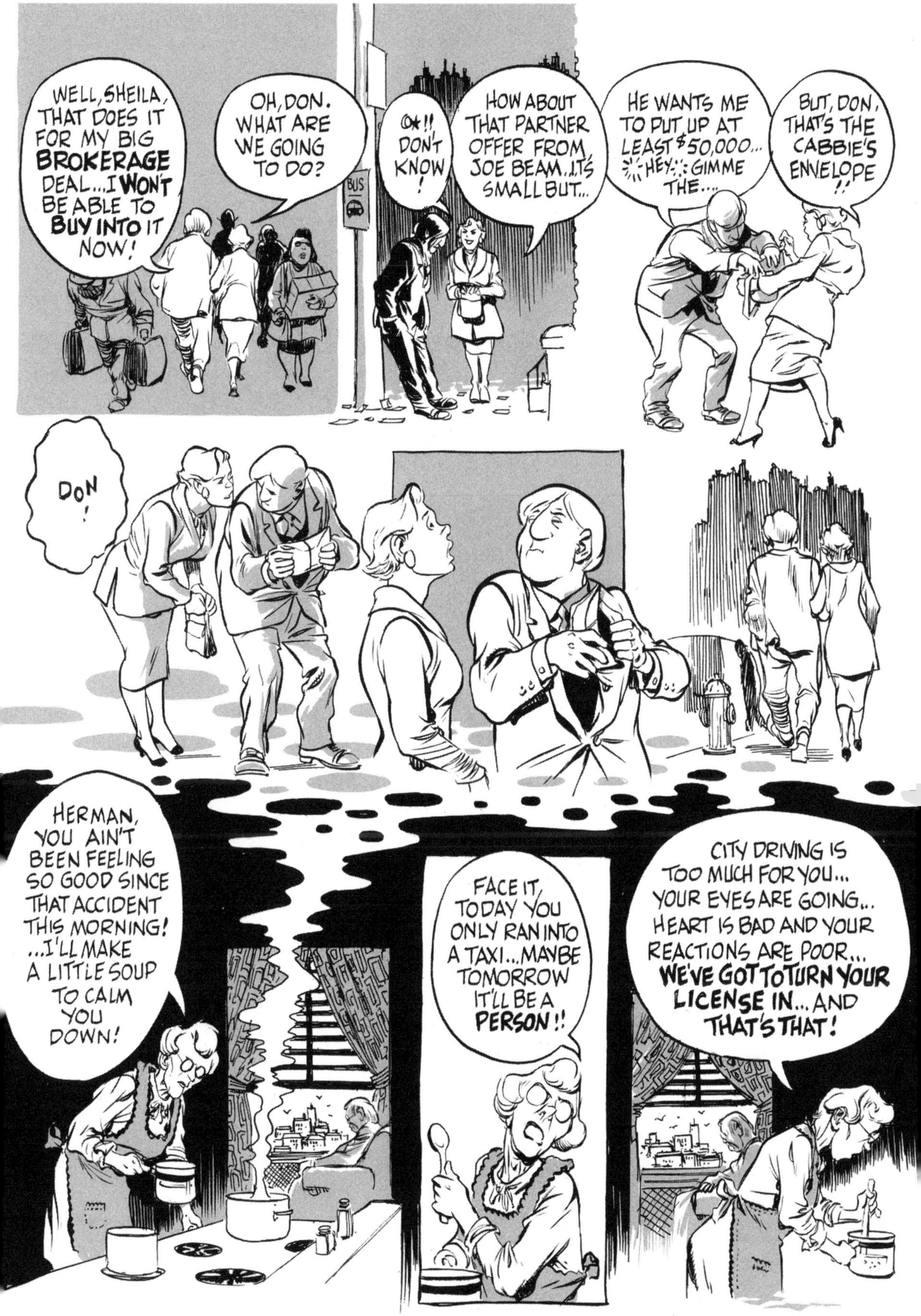
WELL, SHEILA, THAT DOES IT FOR MY BIG BROKERAGE DEAL... I WON'T BE ABLE TO BUY INTO IT NOW!
OH, DON. WHAT ARE WE GOING TO DO?
BUS
@*!! DON'T KNOW!
HOW ABOUT THAT PARTNER OFFER FROM JOE BEAM..IT'S SMALL BUT...
HE WANTS ME TO PUT UP AT LEAST $50,000... HEY GIMME THE...
BUT, DON, THAT'S THE CABBIE'S ENVELOPE!!
DON!
HERMAN, YOU AIN'T BEEN FEELING SO GOOD SINCE THAT ACCIDENT THIS MORNING! ...I'LL MAKE A LITTLE SOUP TO CALM YOU DOWN!
FACE IT, TODAY YOU ONLY RAN INTO A TAXI... MAYBE TOMORROW IT'LL BE A PERSON!!
CITY DRIVING IS TOO MUCH FOR YOU... YOUR EYES ARE GOING... HEART IS BAD AND YOUR REACTIONS ARE POOR... WE'VE GOT TO TURN YOUR LICENSE IN... AND THAT'S THAT!

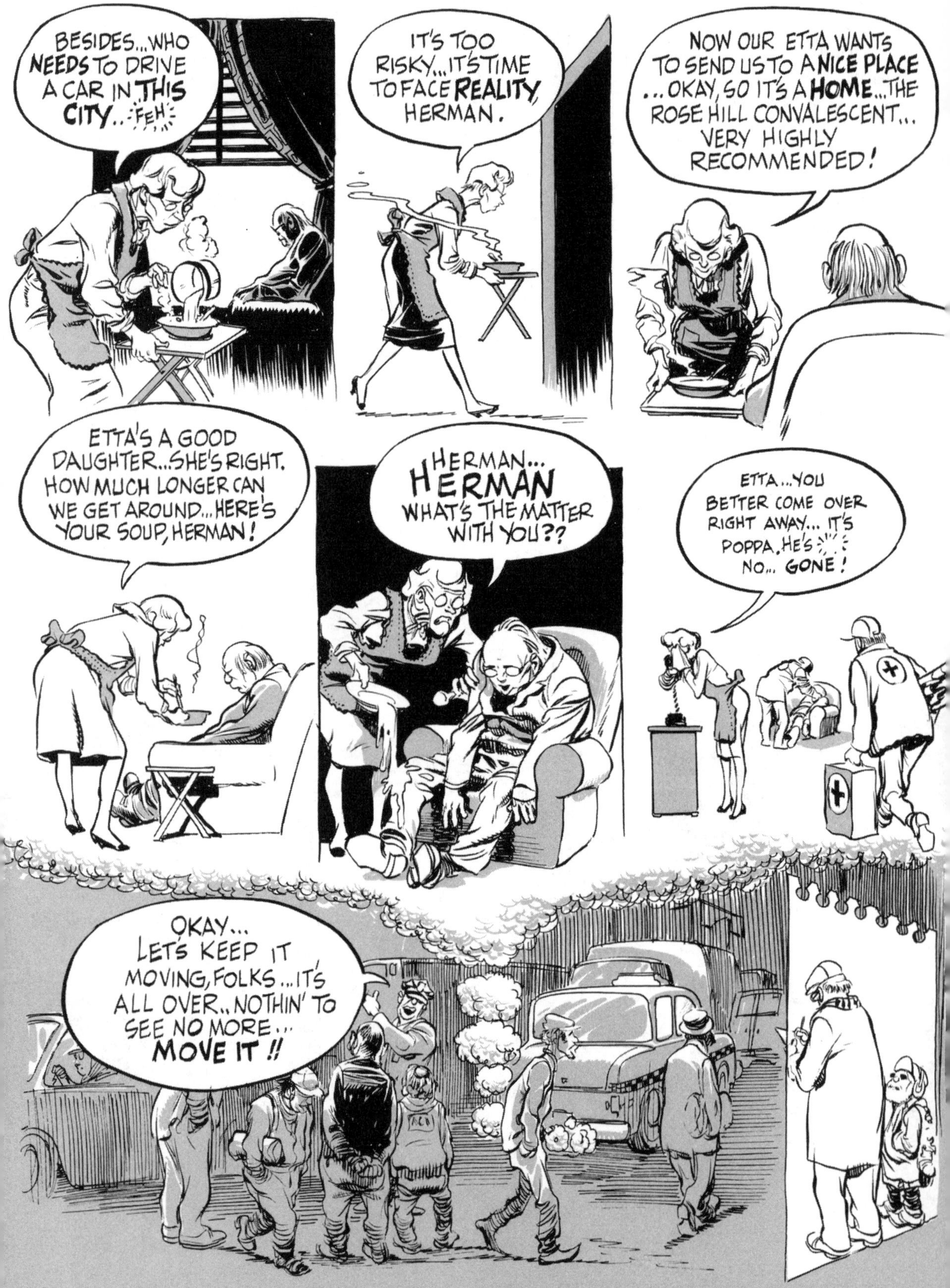
BESIDES...WHO NEEDS TO DRIVE A CAR IN THIS CITY... FEH
IT'S TOO RISKY... IT'S TIME TO FACE REALITY, HERMAN.
NOW OUR ETTA WANTS TO SEND US TO A NICE PLACE ...OKAY, SO IT'S A HOME...THE ROSE HILL CONVALESCENT... VERY HIGHLY RECOMMENDED!
ETTA'S A GOOD DAUGHTER...SHE'S RIGHT. HOW MUCH LONGER CAN WE GET AROUND...HERE'S YOUR SOUP, HERMAN!
HERMAN... HERMAN WHAT'S THE MATTER WITH YOU??
ETTA...YOU BETTER COME OVER RIGHT AWAY... IT'S POPPA. HE'S NO... GONE!
OKAY... LET'S KEEP IT MOVING, FOLKS...IT'S ALL OVER.. NOTHIN' TO SEE NO MORE... MOVE IT!!

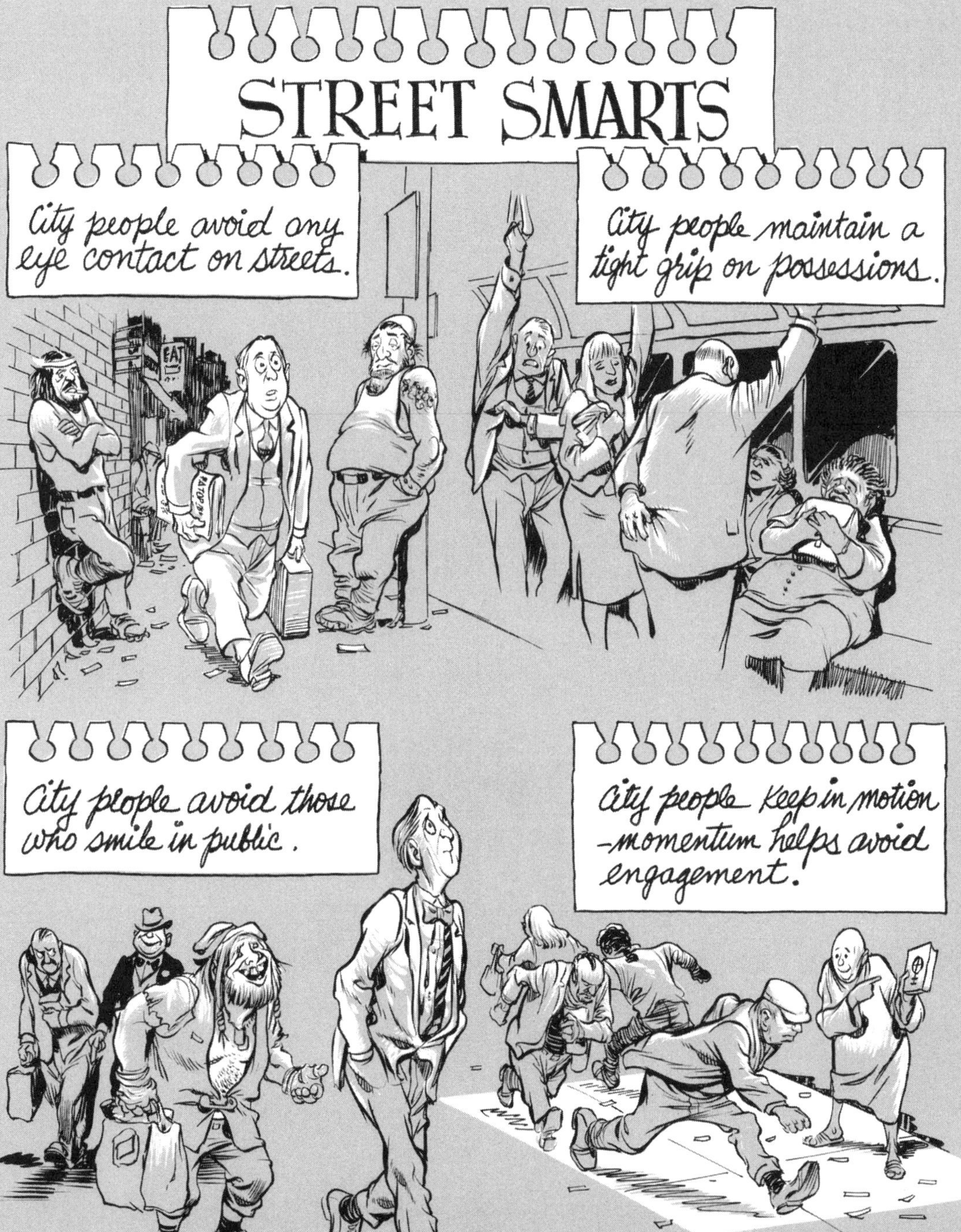

STREET SMARTS
City people avoid any eye contact on streets.
City people maintain a tight grip on possessions.
City people avoid those who smile in public.
City people keep in motion -momentum helps avoid engagement.
EAT

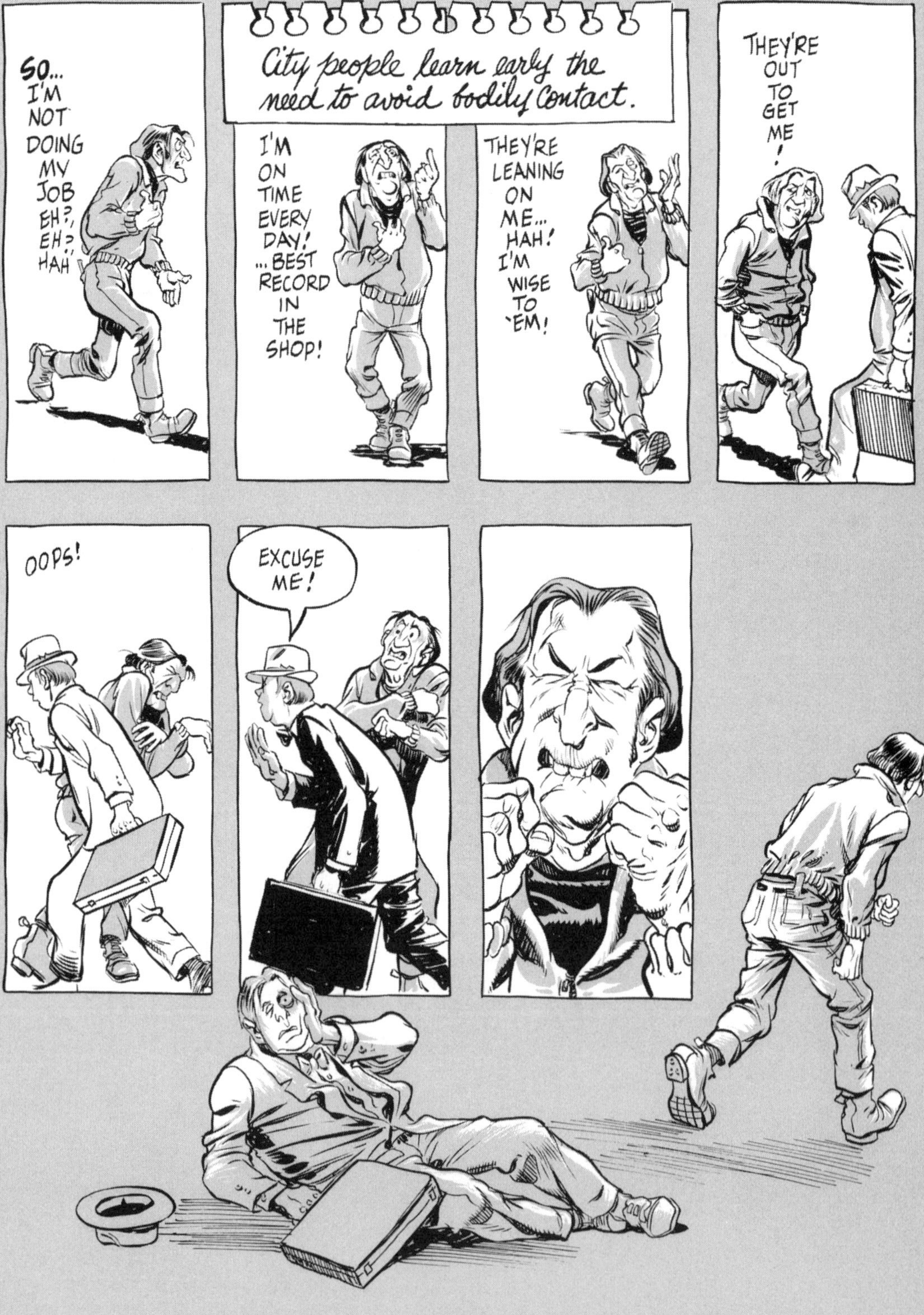
SO... I'M NOT DOING MY JOB EH?, EH?, HAH
City people learn early the need to avoid bodily contact.
I'M ON TIME EVERY DAY! ...BEST RECORD IN THE SHOP!
THEY'RE LEANING ON ME... HAH! I'M WISE TO 'EM!
THEY'RE OUT TO GET ME!
OOPS!
EXCUSE ME!

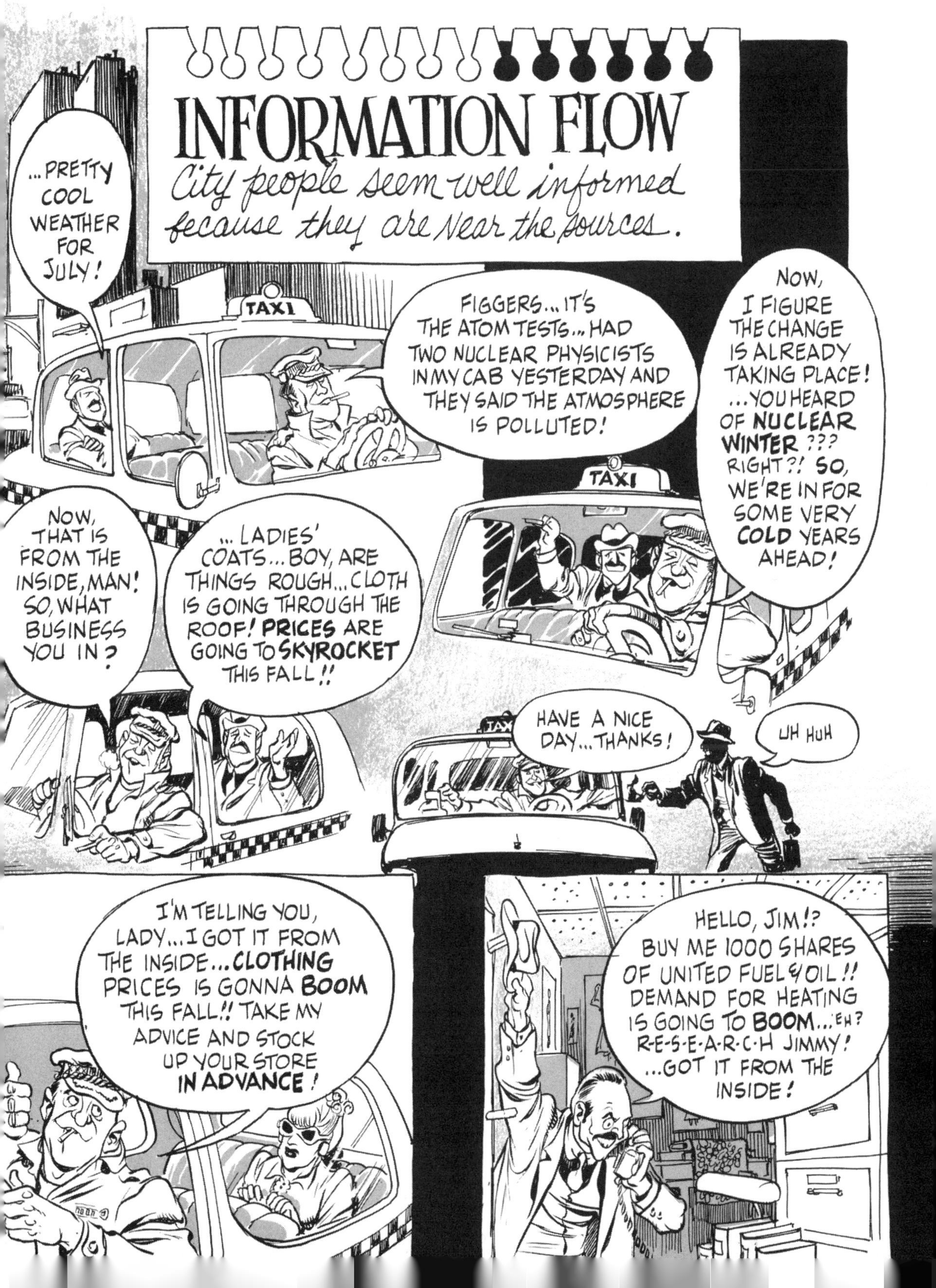
INFORMATION FLOW
City people seem well informed because they are near the sources.
...PRETTY COOL WEATHER FOR JULY!
FIGGERS... IT'S THE ATOM TESTS... HAD TWO NUCLEAR PHYSICISTS IN MY CAB YESTERDAY AND THEY SAID THE ATMOSPHERE IS POLLUTED!
TAXI
NOW, I FIGURE THE CHANGE IS ALREADY TAKING PLACE! ...YOU HEARD OF NUCLEAR WINTER??? RIGHT?! SO, WE'RE IN FOR SOME VERY COLD YEARS AHEAD!
TAXI
NOW, THAT IS FROM THE INSIDE, MAN! SO, WHAT BUSINESS YOU IN?
... LADIES' COATS... BOY, ARE THINGS ROUGH... CLOTH IS GOING THROUGH THE ROOF! PRICES ARE GOING TO SKYROCKET THIS FALL!!
HAVE A NICE DAY... THANKS!
UH HUH
I'M TELLING YOU, LADY... I GOT IT FROM THE INSIDE... CLOTHING PRICES IS GONNA BOOM THIS FALL!! TAKE MY ADVICE AND STOCK UP YOUR STORE IN ADVANCE!
HELLO, JIM!? BUY ME 1000 SHARES OF UNITED FUEL & OIL!! DEMAND FOR HEATING IS GOING TO BOOM... EH? R-E-S-E-A-R-C-H JIMMY! ...GOT IT FROM THE INSIDE!

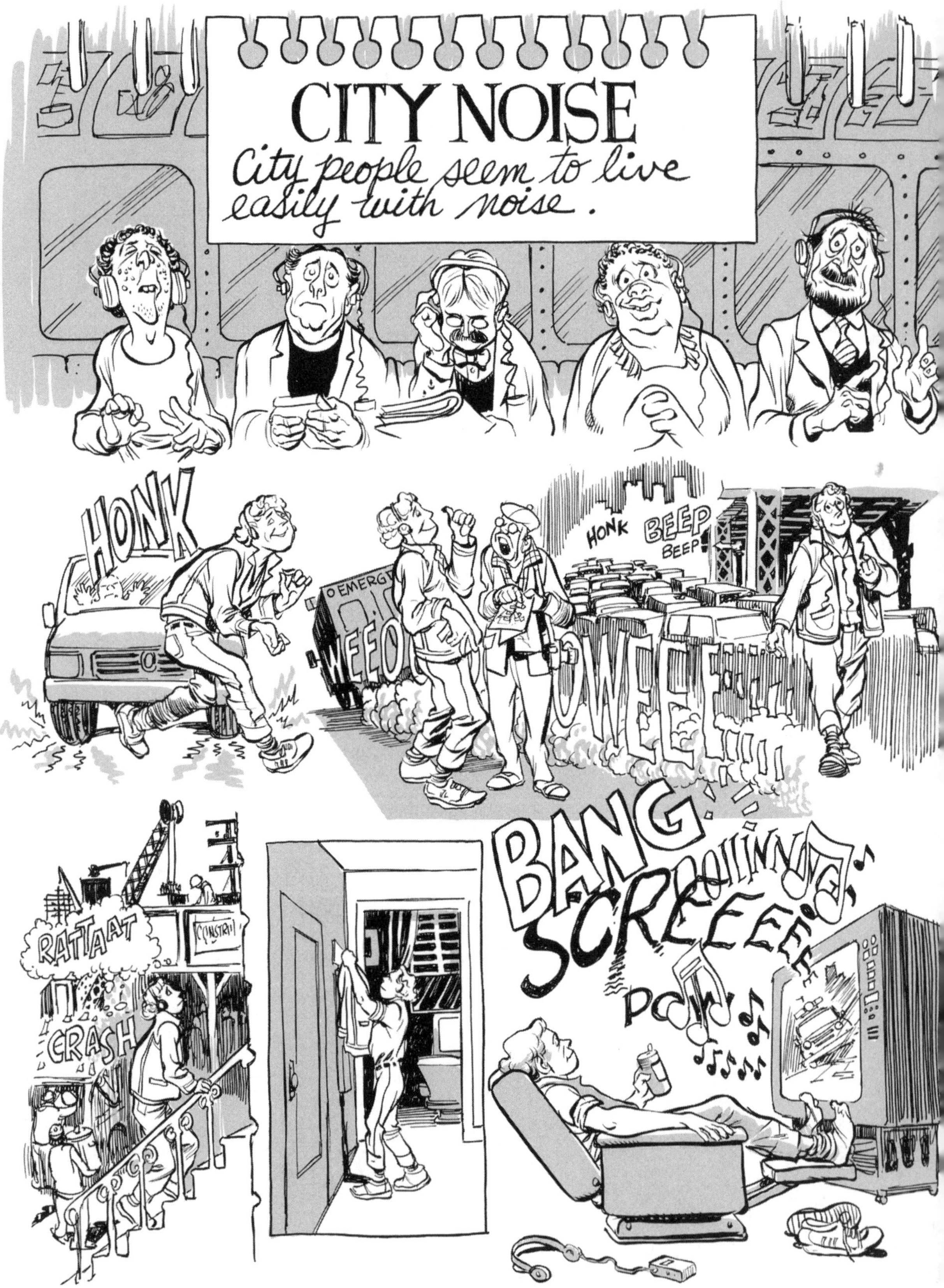
CITY NOISE
City people seem to live easily with noise.
HONK
HONK
BEEP
BEEP
RATTAAT
CRASH
BANG
SCREEEEE
POW

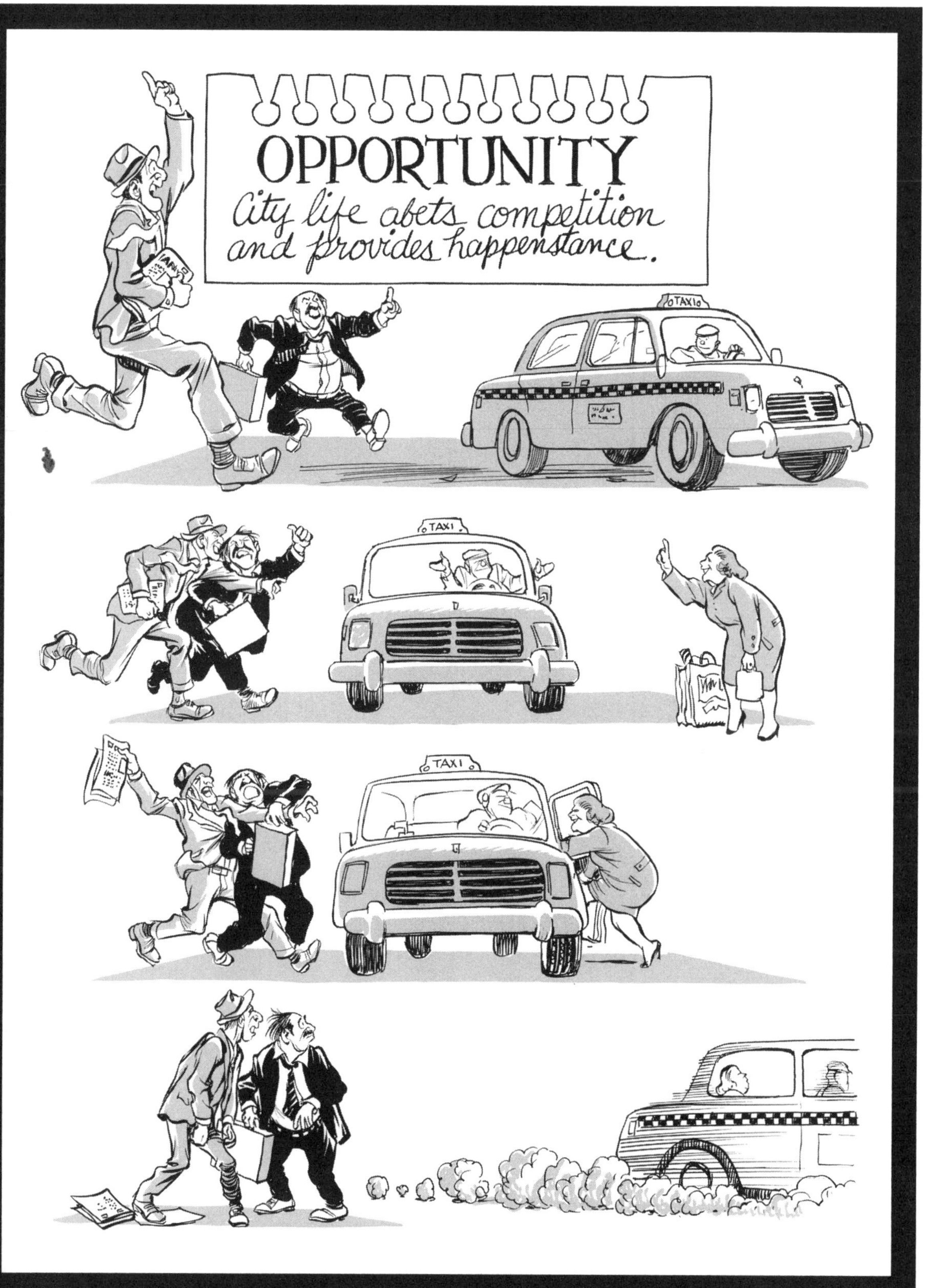

OPPORTUNITY
City life abets competition and provides happenstance.
TAXI
TAXI
TAXI

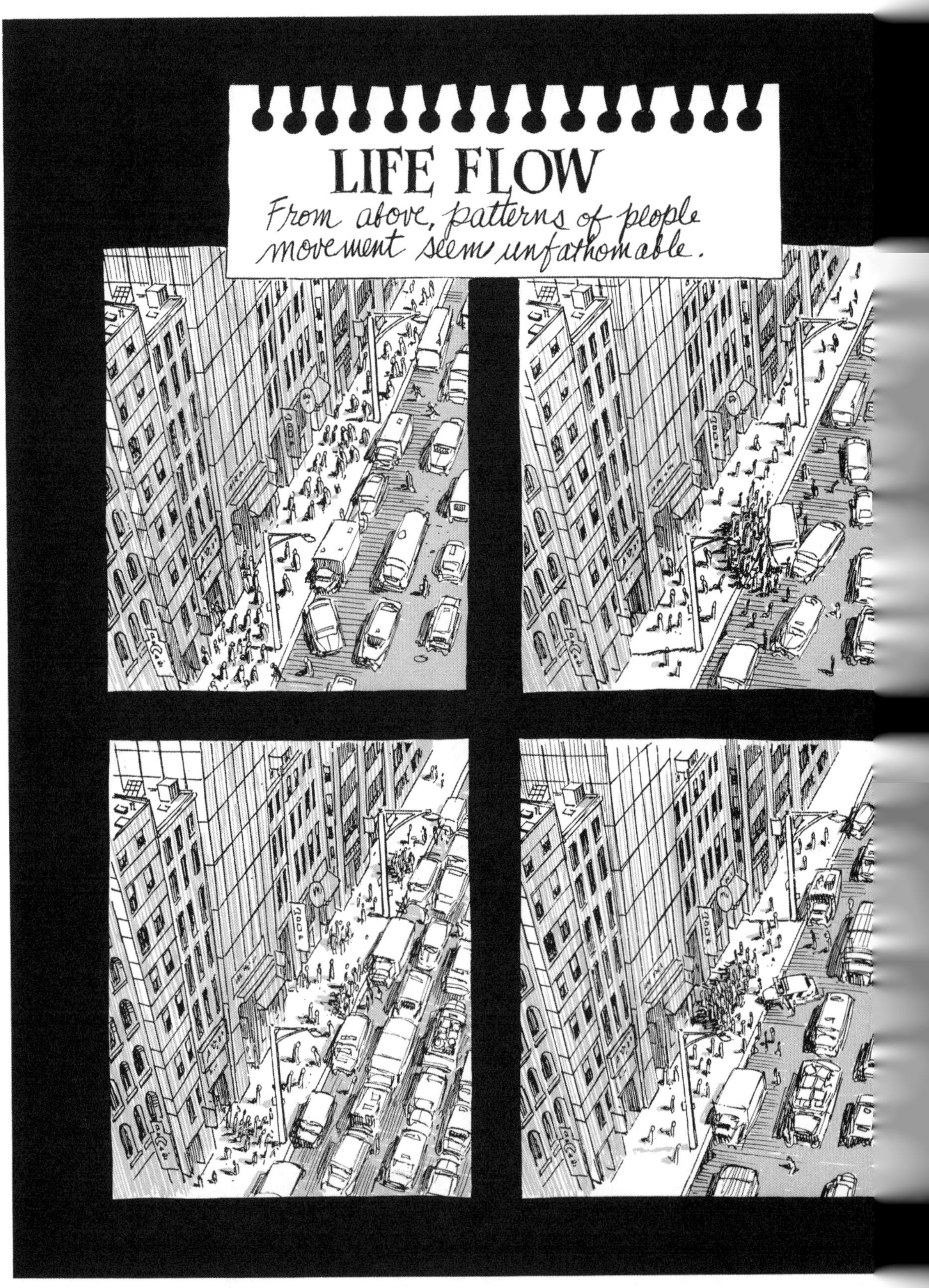
LIFE FLOW
From above, patterns of people movement seem unfathomable.

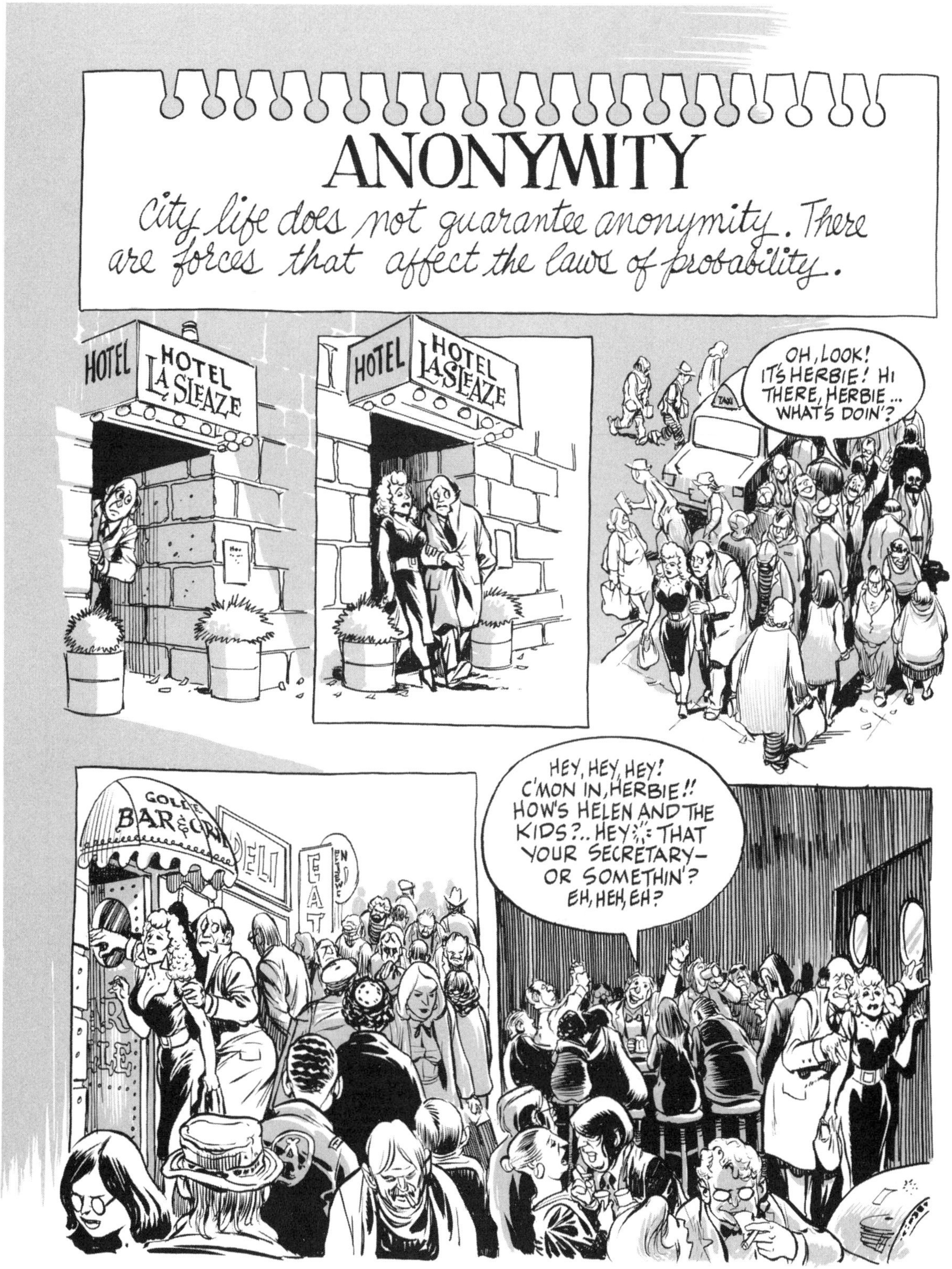
ANONYMITY
City life does not guarantee anonymity. There are forces that affect the laws of probability.
HOTEL
HOTEL LA SLEAZE
HOTEL
HOTEL LA SLEAZE
OH, LOOK! IT'S HERBIE! HI THERE, HERBIE... WHAT'S DOIN'?
TAXI
BAR & GRILL
DELI
EAT
HEY, HEY, HEY! C'MON IN, HERBIE!! HOW'S HELEN AND THE KIDS?.. HEY!! THAT YOUR SECRETARY— OR SOMETHIN'? EH, HEH, EH?

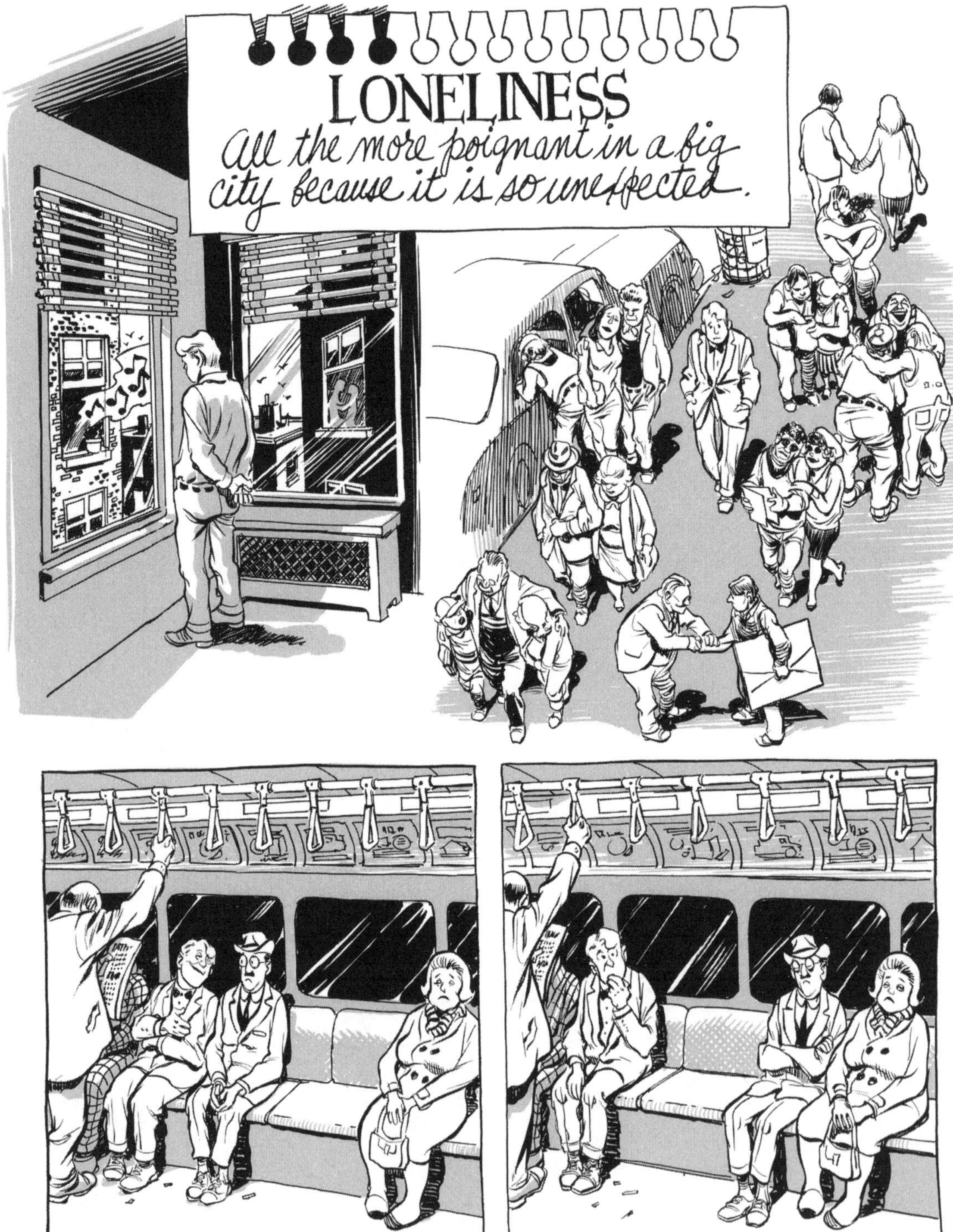
LONELINESS
All the more poignant in a big city because it is so unexpected.

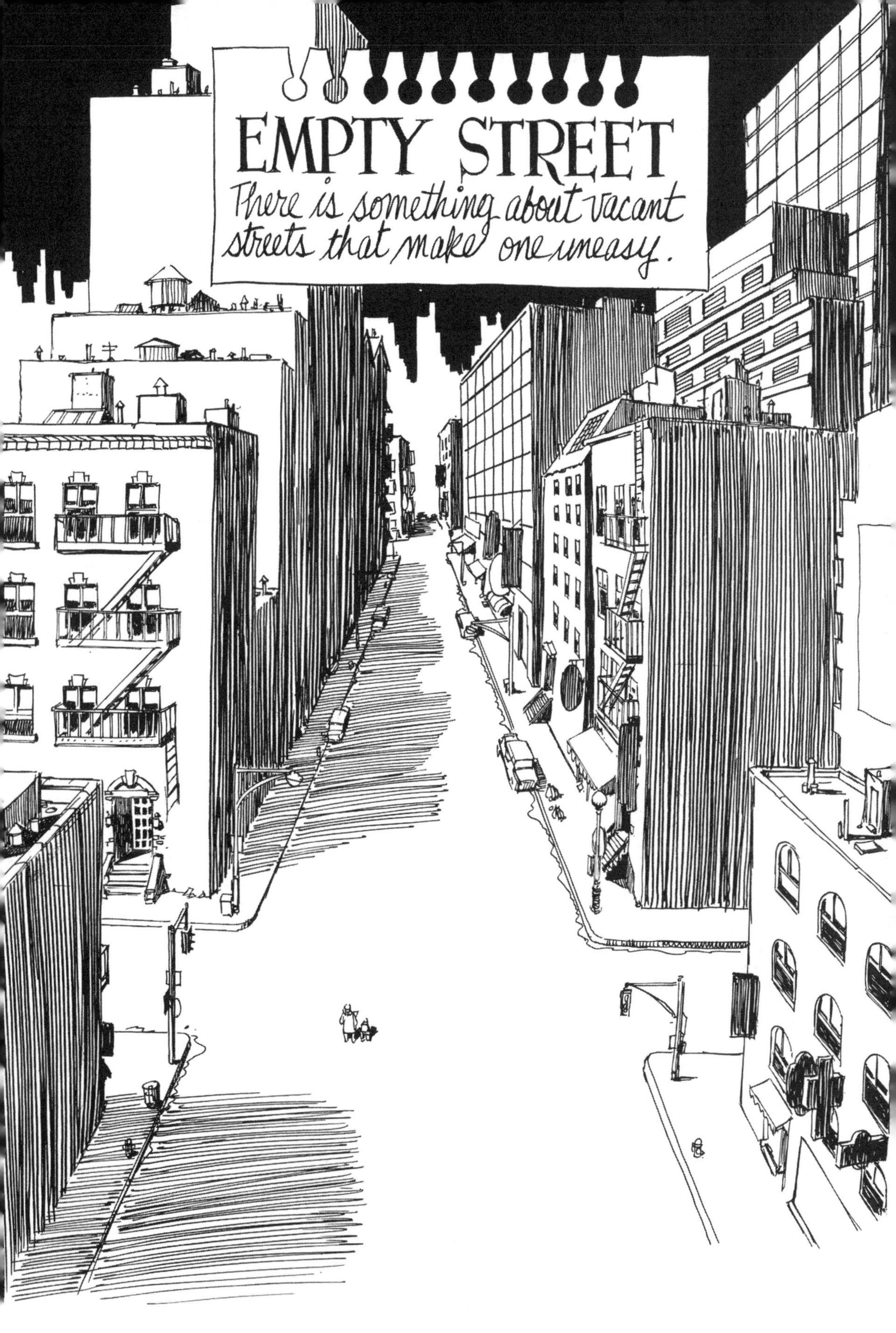
EMPTY STREET
There is something about vacant streets that make one uneasy.

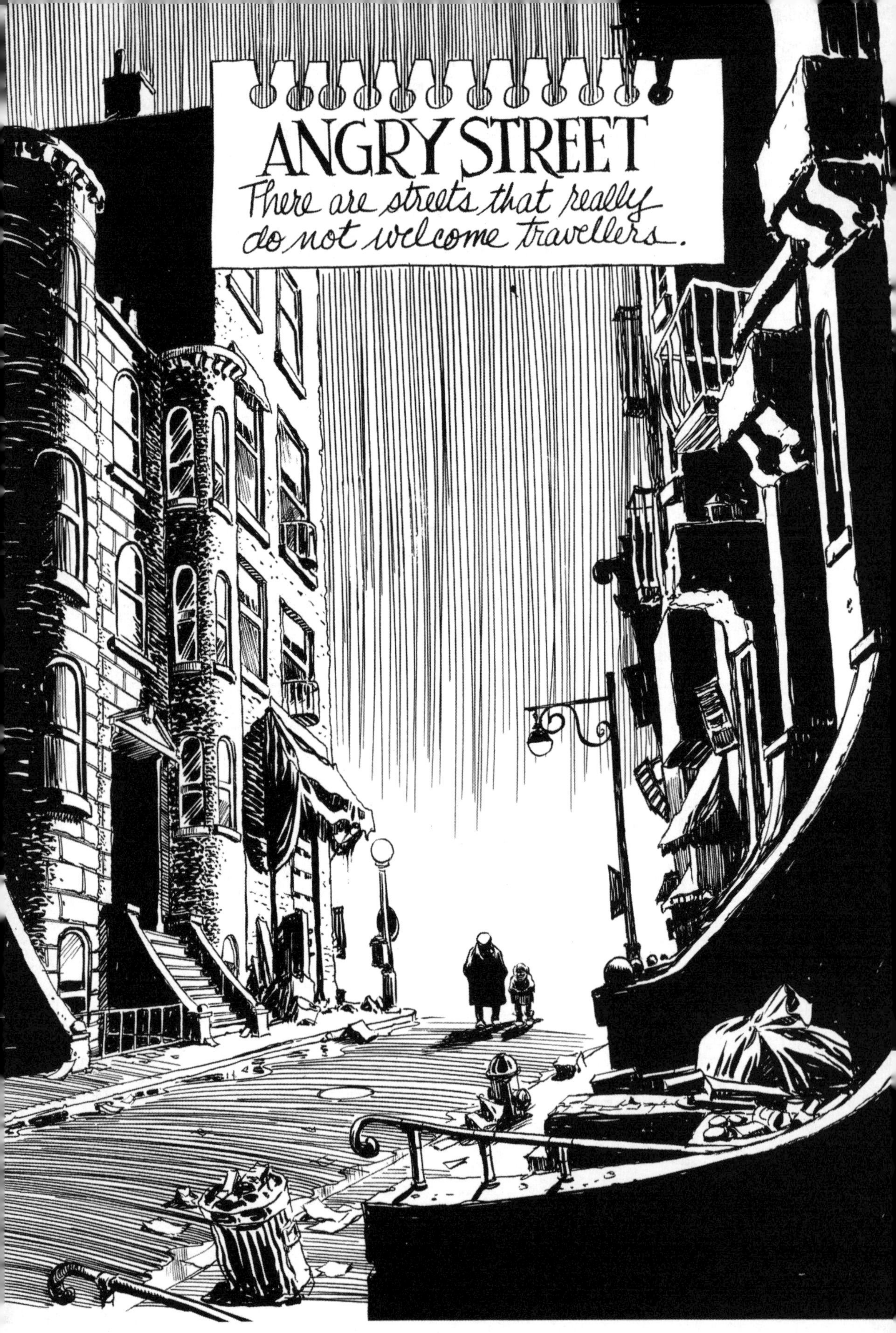
ANGRY STREET
There are streets that really do not welcome travellers.

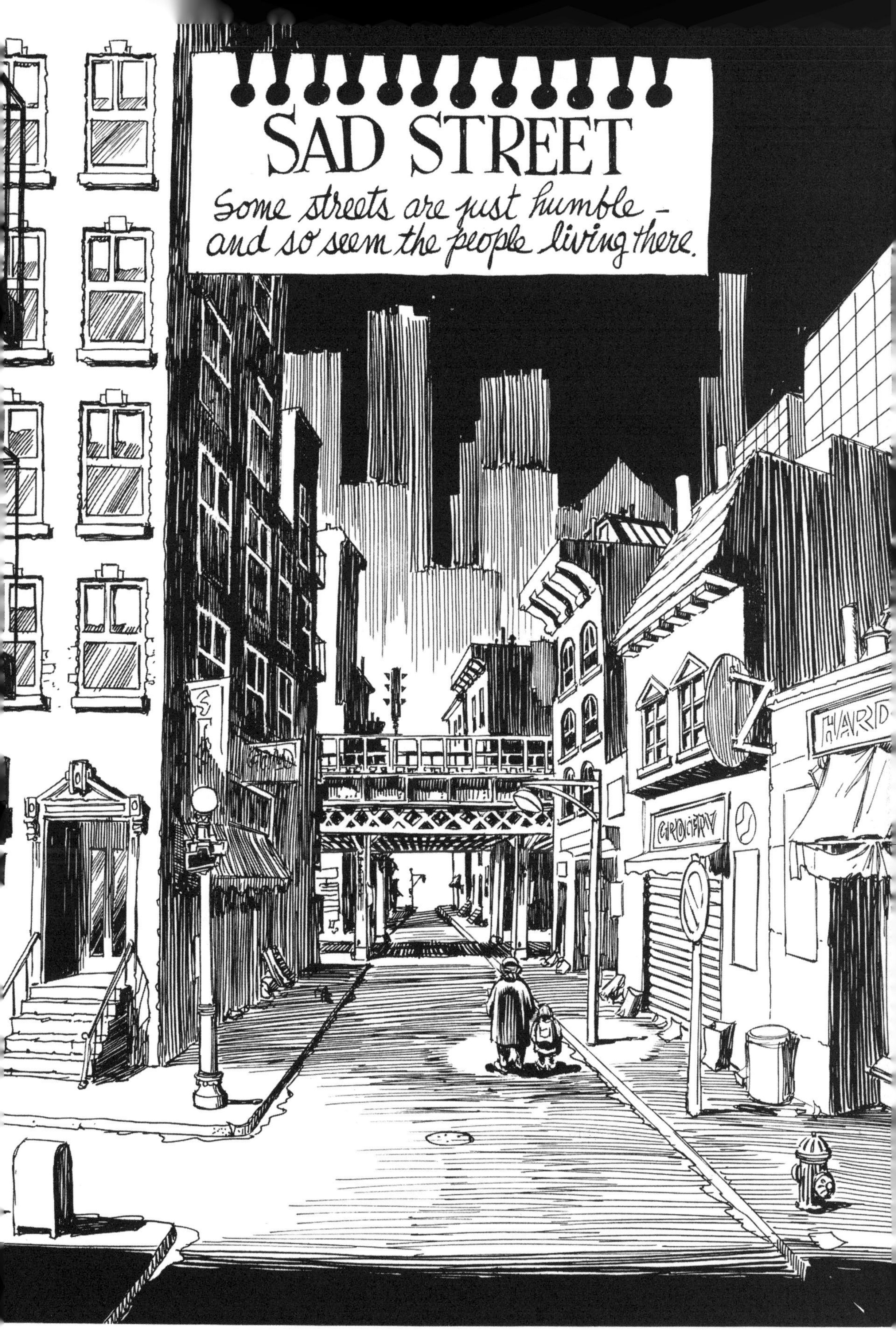
SAD STREET
Some streets are just humble - and so seem the people living there.
HARD
GROCERY

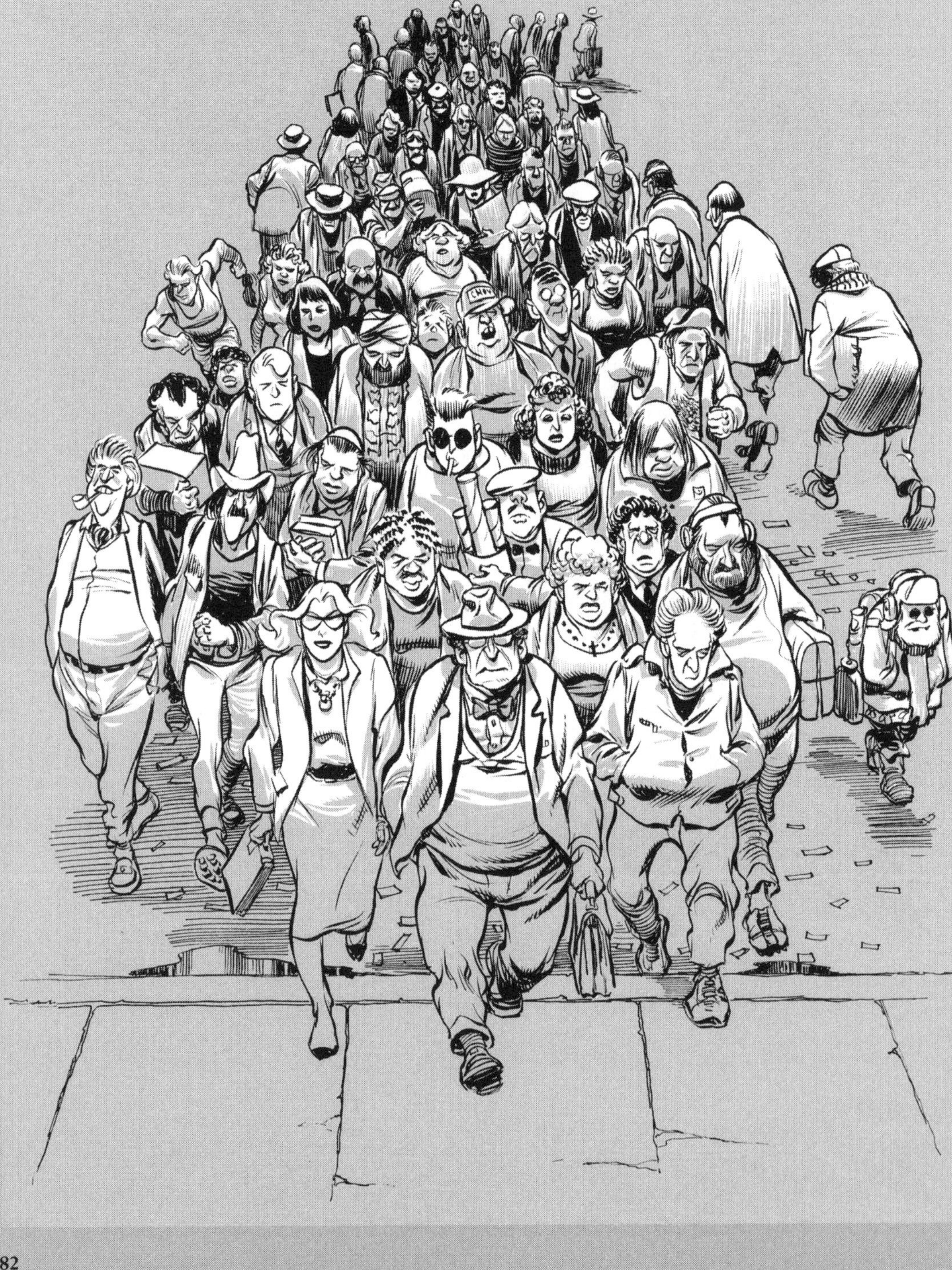

About the Author

Will Eisner (1917–2005) was the grand old man of comics. He was present at the birth of the comic book industry in the 1930s, creating such titles as *Blackhawk* and *Sheena, Queen of the Jungle*. He created *The Spirit* in 1940, syndicating it for twelve years as a unique and innovative sixteen-page Sunday newspaper insert, with a weekly circulation of 5 million copies. In the seven decades since, *The Spirit* has almost never been out of print. As a Pentagon-based warrant officer during World War Two, Eisner pioneered the instructional use of comics, continuing to produce them for the U.S. Army under civilian contract into the 1970s, along with educational comics for clients as diverse as General Motors and elementary school children.

In 1978 Eisner created the first successful "graphic novel," *A Contract With God*, launching a bold new literary genre. Nearly twenty celebrated graphic novels by him followed. Since 1988 the comic industry's top award for excellence has been "The Eisner." He has received numerous honors and awards worldwide, including, ironically, several Eisners and only the second Lifetime Achievement Award bestowed by the National Foundation for Jewish Culture (2002). Michael Chabon's Pulitzer Prize–winning novel *The Amazing Adventures of Kavalier & Clay* is based in good part on Eisner.